THE MEDITATIVE MIND

Ten Dhamma Talks from a
Meditation Retreat
Held in 1987 in Sri Lanka

by
Sister Ayyā Khemā

D1601453

Buddhist Publication Society
P.O. Box 61
54 Sangharaja Mawatha
Kandy, Sri Lanka
http://www.bps.lk

Copyright © 1989 Sister Ayyā Khemā
First edition, called *To Be Seen Here and Now,* 1989
First BPS edition: 2012

Republished with the kind permission of Jhana Verlag

National Library and Documentation Services Board -
Cataloguing-In-Publication Data

Bhikshuni Ayyā Khema,
   The Meditative Mind: Ten Dhamma Talks from a
   Meditation Retreat held in 1987 in Sri Lanka /
   Bhikshuni Ayyā Khemā: ed. by Bhikkhu
   Nyanatusita - Kandy: Buddhist Publication Society
   Inc., 2012
   BP 523s.- 116p.; 18.5cm

   ISBN 978-955-24-0385-9

   i. 294.34435 DDC 23   ii. Title
   iii. Bhikkhu Nyanatusita ed.
   1. Meditation - Buddhism

ISBN: 978-955-24-0385-9

Printed by
Creative Printers & Designers,
Bahirawakanda, Kandy.

Contents

Preface

Meditation retreats are a time for introspection. Because they are held in silence, except for Dhamma talks and questions, the mind becomes more and more used to mindfulness and concentration. This gives added impetus to the hearing of Dhamma, so that the truth of the Buddha's teaching can leave a lasting impression.

When you open this book, dear reader, maybe you could imagine being in a meditation retreat, where nothing else matters except the clarity and wholesomeness of your own mind. This means leaving all daily preoccupations aside and focusing strictly on the wonderful freedom the Buddha's teaching and practice can provide. May you enjoy the following pages and find something useful in them.

Sister Ayyā Khemā
Parappuduwa Nuns' Island,
Dodanduwa,
Sri Lanka.
December 31st, 1989

I. The Meditative Mind

People are often surprised how difficult it is to meditate. Outwardly it seems to be such a simple matter to just sit down on a little pillow and watch one's breath. What could be hard about that? The difficulty lies in the fact that one's whole being is totally unprepared. Our mind, senses, and feelings are used to trade in the market place, namely the world in which we live, but meditation cannot be done in a market place; that is impossible. There is nothing to buy or trade or arrange in meditation, but most people's attitude remains the same as usual and that just does not work.

We need patience with ourselves. It takes time to change to the point where meditation is actually a state of mind, available at any time because the market place is no longer important. The market place does not just mean going shopping. It means everything that is done in the world: all the connections, ideas, hopes and memories, all the rejections and resistances, all our reactions.

In meditation we may have momentary glimpses of concentration (*samādhi*), but they cannot be sustained and our mind slips off and goes right back to where it came from. In order to counteract that, we have to have determination to make our life a meditative one. This does not mean we have to meditate from morning till night—I do not know anyone who does so. It does not mean we cannot fulfil our duties and obligations, because they are necessary and take priority as long as we have them. It means that we watch ourselves carefully in all our actions and reactions to make sure that everything happens in the light of the Dhamma—the Truth. This applies to the smallest detail such as our food and what we listen to or talk about. Only then can the mind be ready with a meditative quality when we sit down on the cushion. It means that no matter where we find ourselves, we remain introspective. That does not mean we cannot talk to others, but we watch the content of the discussion.

That is not easy to do and the mind often slips off but we can become aware of the slip. If we are not even aware that we have digressed from mindfulness and inner watchfulness, we are not on the meditative path yet. If our mind has the Dhamma quality established within, then meditation has a good chance.

The more we know of the Dhamma, the more we can watch whether we comply with its guidelines. There is no blame attached to our inability to do so, but the least we can do is to know the guidelines and know where we are making mistakes. Then we practise to get nearer and nearer to absolute reality, until one day we will actually *be* the Dhamma.

There is this difference between one who knows and one who practises. The one who knows may understand the words and concepts, but the one who practises knows only one thing, namely, to become that truth. Words are an utilitarian means not only for communication, but also to solidify ideas. That is why words can never reveal the truth, only personal experience can. We attain our experiences through realising what's happening within and why it is as it is. This means that we combine watchfulness with inquiry as to why we are thinking, saying and reacting the way we do. Unless we use our mind in this way, meditation will be an on-again, off-again affair and will remain difficult. When meditation does not bring joy, most people are quite happy to forget about it.

Without the meditative mind and experience, the Dhamma cannot arise in the heart, because the Dhamma is not in words. The Buddha was able to verbalise his inner experience for our benefit, to give us a guideline. That means we can find a direction, but we have to do the travelling ourselves.

To have a meditative mind, we need to develop some important inner qualities. We already have their seed within otherwise we couldn't cultivate them. If we want flowers in our garden and there are no seeds, we can water and fertilise, yet nothing will grow. The watering and fertilising of the mind is done in meditation. Weeding has to be done in daily living. Weeds always seem to grow better in any garden than the flowers do. It takes a lot of strength to uproot those weeds, but it is not so difficult to cut them down. As they get cut down again and again, they eventually become feeble and their uprooting is made easier. Cutting down and uprooting the weeds needs sufficient introspection into ourselves to know what a weed is and what is a flower. We have to be very sure, because we do not want to pull out all the flowers and leave all the weeds. A garden with many weeds is not much of an ornament.

People's hearts and minds usually contain equal amounts of flowers and weeds. We are born with the three roots of evil: greed, hate and delusion, and the three roots of good: generosity, loving-kindness and wisdom. Does not it make sense to try and get rid of those three roots which are the generators of all problems, all our unpleasant experiences and reactions?

If we want to eliminate those three roots, we have to look at their manifestations. Roots are underneath the surface, but obviously a root sprouts and shows itself above the surface as a weed. We can see that within ourselves. Caused by delusion, we manifest greed and hate. There are different facets of greed and hate, and the simplest and most common one is "I like," "I want," "I do not like," and "I do not want." Most people think such reactions are perfectly justified, and yet it is greed and hate. Our roots have sprouted in so many different ways that we have all sorts of weeds growing. In a garden we will find possibly thirty or forty different types of weeds. We might have that many or more unwholesome thoughts and emotions. They have different appearances and power but they are all coming from the same roots. As we cannot get at the roots yet, we have to deal with what is above the surface. When we cultivate the good roots, they become so mighty and strong that the weeds do not find enough nourishment any more. As long as we allow room for the weeds in our garden, we take the nutrients away from the beautiful plants, instead of cultivating those more and more. This cultivation of good inner qualities takes place as a development in daily living, which then makes it possible to meditate as a natural outcome of our state of mind.

Now we are trying to change our mind from an ordinary one to a meditative one, which is difficult if one has not practised very much yet. We only have one mind and carry that around with us to every activity and also to the meditation. If we have an inkling that meditation can bring us peace and happiness, then we need to make sure we have a meditative mind already when we sit down. To change it from busyness to quiet at that moment is too difficult.

The state of mind which we need to develop for meditation is well described by the Buddha. Two aspects of importance are mindfulness (*sati*) and the calming of the senses. Internal mindfulness may sometimes be exchanged for external mindfulness because under some circumstances that is an essential part of practice. The world impinges upon us, which we cannot deny.

External mindfulness also means to see a tree, for instance, in a completely new way. Not with the usual thoughts of "that is pretty," or "I like this one in my garden," but rather noticing that there are live and dead leaves, that there are growing plants, mature ones and dying ones. We can witness the growth, birth and decay all around us. We can understand craving very clearly by watching ants, mosquitoes, dogs. We need not look at them as a nuisance, but as teachers. Ants, mosquitoes and barking dogs are the kind of teachers who do not leave us alone until the lessons are fully learned. When we see all in the light of birth, decay, death, greed, hate and delusion, we are looking in a mirror of all life around us; then we have Dhamma on show. All of us are proclaiming the truth of Dhamma constantly, only we do not pay enough attention.

We can use mindfulness to observe that everything in existence consists of the four elements, earth, fire, water, air; and then check out what is the difference between ourselves and all else. When we take practice seriously and look at all life in such a way, then we find the truth all around as well as within us. Nothing else exists.

This gives us the ability to leave the marketplace behind where the mind flits from one thing to the next, never has a moment's peace, is either dull and indifferent or hateful and greedy. But when we look at that which really is, we are drawing nearer to what the Buddha taught, out of his compassion for all the beings that are roaming around in samsara from one state of unsatisfactoriness or suffering (*dukkha*) to the next. He taught the truth of Dhamma so that people like us may awaken to it.

We should neither believe nor disbelieve what we hear or read, but try it out ourselves. If we give our wholehearted attention to this practice, we will find that it changes our approach to living and dying. Wholeheartedness is necessary to succeed in anything we do. If we get married and are half-hearted about it, that cannot be very successful. Half-hearted practice of Dhamma results in chaotic misunderstanding. Wholeheartedness may have at its core devotion, and a mind which goes beyond everyday thoughts and activities.

Another facet which goes together with mindfulness (*sati*) is clear comprehension (*sampajañña*).

Mindfulness is to be aware only, without any discriminating faculty. Mindfulness does not evaluate or judge but pays full attention. Clear comprehension has four aspects or steps to it. The first is, "What is my purpose in thinking, talking or doing?" Thought, speech and action are our three doors. The second is, "Am I using the most skilful means for my purpose?" That needs wisdom and discrimination. The third is, "Are these means within the Dhamma?" It is necessary to know the distinction between the wholesome and the unwholesome. The thought process needs our primary attention, because speech and action will follow from it. Sometimes people think that the end justifies the means. It does not. Both means and end have to be within the Dhamma. The fourth step is to check whether our purpose has been accomplished, and if not, why not.

If we live with these steps in mind, we will slow down, which is helpful for our reactions. I do not suggest inactivity, that is not the answer, but to maintain the meditative quality of the mind, which watches over what we are doing. When we use mindfulness and clear comprehension, we have to give time to investigate. Checking prevents mistakes.

Our wrong thinking creates the danger of making bad kamma and takes us away from the truth into nebulous mind-states. The Dhamma is straight forward, simple and pure. It needs a pure mind to stay with it. Otherwise we find ourselves outside of it again and again.

External mindfulness can also extend to other people, but here we need to be very careful. Seeing and knowing others engenders negative judgment. If we practise external mindfulness towards other people, we have to realise that judging others is making bad kamma. We can pay attention with compassion. People-watching is one of the most popular pastimes but usually done with the intention of finding fault. Everyone who is not enlightened has faults; even the highly developed non-returner (*anāgāmi*) has yet five fetters to lose. What to say about ordinary worldlings? To use other people as our mirror is very helpful because they reflect our own being. We can only see in others what we already know about ourselves. The rest is lost to us.

If we add clear comprehension to our mindfulness and check our purpose and skilful means we will eliminate much grief and worry. We will develop an awareness which will make every day, every moment an adventure. Most people feel bogged down and burdened. Either they have too much or too little to do; not enough money to do what they like or they frantically move about trying to occupy themselves. Everybody wants to escape from unsatisfactory conditions, but the escape mechanism that each one chooses does not provide real inner joy. However with mindfulness and clear comprehension, just watching a tree is fascinating. It brings a new dimension to our life, a buoyancy of mind, enabling us to grasp wholeness, instead of the limitations of our family, job, hopes and dreams. That way we can expand, because we are fascinated with what we see around and within us, and want to explore further. We do not watch "my" mind, "my" body, "my" tree, but watch just phenomena all around us that provide us with the most fascinating, challenging schoolroom that anybody could ever find. Our interest in the schoolroom increases as mindfulness increases.

To develop a meditative mind, we also need to calm our senses. We do not have to deny ourselves sensory experiences, that would be foolishness, but see them for what they are. Māra the tempter is not a fellow with a long tail and a flaming red tongue, but rather our senses. We hardly ever pay attention to what they do to us when they pull us from an interesting sight to a beautiful sound, and back to the sight, the thought, the idea. No Peace! Our constant endeavour is to catch a moment's pleasure.

A sense contact has to be very fleeting, because otherwise it becomes a great dukkha. Let's say we are offered a very nice meal, which tastes extremely good. So we say to our host: "That is a very nice meal, I like it very much." The host replies: "I have lots of food here, please stay around and eat for another two or three hours." If we did, we would not only get sick in body but also disgusted in our mind. A meal can last twenty or at the most thirty minutes. Each taste contact can only last a second and then we have to chew and swallow. If we were to keep it in the mouth any longer, it would become very unpleasant.

Maybe we feel very hot and go to take a cold shower. We say to our friend waiting outside: "Now I feel good, that cold water is very pleasant." Our friend says, "We have plenty of cold water, you can have a shower for the next five to six hours." Nothing but absolute misery would result. We can enjoy a cold shower for ten or twenty minutes at the most.

Anything that is prolonged will create dukkha. All contacts pass quickly, because that is their nature. The same goes for sight, our eyes are continually blinking. We cannot even keep sight constant for the length of time we are looking at anything. We may be looking at a beautiful painting for a little while and really like it. Someone says: "You can stay here and look at the painting for the next five hours; we are not closing the museum yet." Nobody could do that. We cannot look at the same thing a long time, without feeling bored, losing all awareness, or even falling asleep. Sense contacts are not only limited because of their inability to give satisfaction. They are actually waves that come and go. If we are listening to some lovely music, after a few hours the same music becomes unbearable. Our sense contacts are mirroring a reflection of satisfaction, which has no real basis in fact. That is Māra constantly leading us astray.

There is a pertinent story of a monk in the Buddha's time which relates the ultimate in sense discipline: A married couple had a big row and the woman decided to run away. She put on her best sari, wore all her gold jewellery and left to go to her relatives. On the way she saw a monk walking on the street, at whom she laughed. The monk looked up and only saw her teeth. After a while the husband was sorry that he had let her go and followed her. He ran here and there, but couldn't find her. Finally he came across the monk. He asked the monk if he'd seen a woman in a red sari with long black hair and lots of jewellery. The monk said: "I only saw a set of teeth going by."

The monk was not paying attention to the concepts of a woman with long black hair, a red sari, and lots of jewellery, but only to the fact that there was a human being with a set of teeth. He had calmed his senses to the point where the sight object was no longer tempting him into a reaction. An ordinary person at the sight of a beautiful woman with black hair, a red sari and lots of jewellery, going excitedly along the street, might have been tempted to follow her. A set of teeth going by, is highly unlikely to create desire. That way of paying attention is calming the senses.

If we come upon a snake, it is not an object of dislike or destruction, but just a sentient being that happens to be around. That is all. There is nothing to be done, nothing to react to. If we think of it as a snake that could kill us, then of course, the mind can go berserk, just as the monk's mind could have done, if he had thought "Oh, what a beautiful woman."

If we watch our senses again and again, this becomes a habit, and is no longer difficult. Life will be much more peaceful. The world as we know it consists of so much proliferation (*papañca*). Everywhere are different colours, shapes, beings and nature's growth. Each family of tree has hundreds of species and sub-species. Nature proliferates. All of us look different. If we do not guard our senses, this proliferation in the world will keep us attracted life after life. There is too much to see, do, know and react to. Since there is no end to all of that we might as well stop and delve inside of ourselves.

A meditative mind is achieved through mindfulness, clear comprehension and calming the senses. These three aspects of practice need to be done in everyday life. Peace and harmony will result, and our meditation will flourish.

II. Skilful Means

The two aspects of our being are mind and body. We have to pay attention to both of them, even though meditation is a mind exercise, not a body exercise.

Some of the most common questions are: "How am I going to learn to sit?" "How am I not going to have any pain?" That is only possible through continued application, doing it again and again. In the beginning, the body just does not like sitting cross-legged on the floor.

We can use this situation as skilful means. When discomfort arises in the body, we learn to pay attention to the mind's reaction, and do not move automatically. Everybody in the world is trying to get out of any kind of discomfort with an instinctive, immediate reaction. It is not that we are not going to get out of discomfort, but in order to make meditation pay off, we have to learn to get out of instinctive, immediate reactions. It is those that land us in dukkha over and over again.

When there is an uncomfortable feeling, it is essential to realise what is happening within. We notice that there is a sense contact, in this case "touch!" The body is making contact, the knees with the cushion, the legs with each other—several contacts are happening. From all sense contacts, feelings arise. There is no way out of that, this is how human beings are made. The Buddha taught cause and effect, that dependent upon any sense contact, feeling results. There are three kinds of feelings, pleasant, unpleasant and neutral. We can forget about the neutral ones, because we are hardly ever aware of them. Neutral is actually considered pleasant, because at least it does not hurt. From this particular touch contact that is being made through the sitting posture, there arises, after a while, an unpleasant feeling. The immediate reaction is to move. Do not! Investigate! By getting to know our own mind, we get to know the world and the universe. All minds contain the seed of enlightenment. Unless we know our own mind, we cannot develop and cultivate that seed. Here the mind has been contacted with an unpleasant feeling, our perception says: "this is painful." Next arise the mental formations (*saṅkhāra*), which are also kamma formations, because we make kamma through our thought processes.

First comes the sense contact, secondly feeling arises. Then perception, the naming of this feeling , followed by dislike. At the moment of dislike, there is the running away through changing our position. That is the kamma making aspect. This is minor negative kamma, yet it is negative, because the mind is in a state of ill will by saying "I do not like it."

The mind may start all kinds of rationalisations: "I wish I'd brought my own little chair"; "I cannot sit"; "At my age I shouldn't do things like this"; "Meditation is too difficult." None of these rationalisations have any intrinsic validity; they are only a mind reacting to an unpleasant feeling. Unless we become acquainted with our mind's reactions, we are not using meditation in the most beneficial manner.

Knowing the unpleasant feeling, we can now try to acquaint ourselves with its true nature. Our whole

life is lived according to our feelings. Unless we become
aware of our reactions to feelings, we remain half
asleep. There is a beautiful little book on this by Thich
Nhat Han called *The Miracle of Being Awake.*[1] This
miracle is nothing but mindfulness, knowing what's
going on within. When we have realised we want to get
rid of the unpleasant feeling, then we can try to disown
it for a moment. Only the Arahant is fully capable of
complete detachment, but we can do so for a short
time. The unpleasant feeling has arisen without our
asking for it and we do not have to believe it to be ours.
We can let it be just a feeling.

If we do that for a moment, we can get back to the
meditation subject (*kammaṭṭhāna*), and have won a
victory over our own negative reactions. Otherwise we
are letting our unpleasant feelings rule us in whatever
way they want. The whole of humanity runs after
pleasant feelings, and away from unpleasant ones.
Unless we at least know that, we have no reference point
for inner change. It may not be possible to reverse that
reaction yet, but at least we know it is happening.

After we have become aware of our mind's
intention, we are free to move and change our sitting
position. There is nothing wrong with changing one's
posture but there is something wrong with instinctive,
impetuous habits. Meditation means total awareness.
Being awake is not the opposite of being asleep; it is the
opposite of being dull and foggy. Such mind states are
mostly due to an unwillingness to look at our
own dukkha. We'd rather hide in a fog. In meditation

---

1. The Wheel Publication Nos. 234–236; BPS, Kandy.

that won't do. The Buddha said that this body is a cancer; the body as a whole is a disease, and we can experience that when just sitting still, it becomes uncomfortable.

Meditation means *samatha* and *vipassanā*, calm and insight. Unless we know the limitations of each and also their possibilities, we won't be able to make good use of the practice. We are generally applying both of them in every session, but we must be able to distinguish between them. If there is no understanding of what's happening in the mind, the fog settles down in it.

Everybody would like bliss, peace and happiness. That is a natural wish. They are available in meditation, with a lot of practice, and some good kamma. However they are not the goal of meditation. The goal of meditation is insight. Yet skilful means for gaining insight are needed and are found in tranquillity meditation.

Making use of a meditation subject, the mind, after some training, will be able to stay on it for a while. Presuming that the mind is able to focus on the breath for even a short time, we realise afterwards that some peace arose, because the mind was not thinking. The thinking process in everybody's mind is hardly ever profound. It is just thinking. Just as the body breathes, so the mind keeps churning. And it keeps churning out mostly irrelevant, unsubstantial and unimportant details, without which we would be much happier.

The mind in its natural state is pure, clear and lucid, luminous, pliable and expandable. Our thinking is the impurity and the blockage. There is hardly a person who does not think all day long, probably without even being aware of it. But when we start meditating, we do become aware of our inner restlessness. We realise we cannot keep the mind on the meditation subject, because we are thinking instead of meditating. The moment we experience our thinking habit (even that takes time to realise) we accomplish two things. We become aware of our mind's activity and also the content of our thoughts. We will realise immediately that our thinking is irrelevant and makes little or no sense. Because of that, we can let go of it fairly easily and return to the meditation subject. We have to be able to stand back and watch the thinking process and not get involved in it. Otherwise we will just keep on thinking instead of meditating.

The mind is the greatest and most delicate tool existing in the universe. All of us have it, but few look after it properly. Practically everybody is interested in looking after their bodies. Eating, sleeping, washing, exercising, seeing the doctor when the body is sick, cutting our hair and nails, filling teeth, doing everything that is necessary to keep the body functioning well. In reality, the body is the servant and the mind is the master. So we are looking after the servant and forgetting the master. If we do that in our homes, we create chaos. That is one of the reasons why the world looks as chaotic as it does. People kill each other, steal from each other and are unfaithful, lie, gossip and slander. Most have absolutely no ideas that the mind is our most precious asset. It gives us wealth beyond compare and yet we do not know how to look after it.

We have to do exactly the same thing for the mind as we do for the body. We need to give it a rest. Imagine if we didn't go to sleep for three or four days, how would we feel? Without energy, without strength, pretty terrible. The body needs a rest, but the mind does too. During the day it thinks, at night it dreams. It is always busy. The only real rest it can ever get, which energises and gives the needed boost to become clear and lucid, is to stay on the meditation subject.

The mind needs a clean-up, which means purification. This happens when all thinking is stopped for a while because of one-pointed concentration. One moment of concentration is one moment of purification. At that time the mind cannot contain ill will or sensual desire or any other negativity. When concentration ceases, the mind reverts to its usual behaviour again. In meditation we can experience that a purified mind gives us happiness, and quite naturally we will try to keep that purification process going also in daily living.

The mind needs the kind of exercise that is not geared towards winning or achieving anything, but just to obey. When we ask the mind to stay on the meditation subject, yet it runs away from it, we know immediately that we are not the master of our mind but that the mind does what it pleases. When we have realised that, we will be less likely to believe our own views and opinions, particularly when they are unwholesome, because we understand that the mind is simply thinking habitually. Only through the meditation process can we become aware of that.

The mind also requires the right kind of food. Because in meditation we can reach states of higher consciousness, we are thereby able to nourish the mind in a way which cannot happen in the ordinary thinking process. Tranquillity meditation leads the mind into realms which are totally unavailable to us otherwise. Happiness and peacefulness arise without dependence on outer conditions, which give us a new freedom.

The mind of every human being contains the seed of Nibbāna. We need training in order to realise what is obscuring our vision. Then the seed can be cultivated and nurtured to full growth. Because our minds contain such a potential, they also contain the peace and happiness which everybody wants. Most people try to find fulfilment through acquiring material objects, seeing or touching, eating or knowing them. Particularly having more and keeping it all safe.

This dependency is a guarantee for dukkha. As long as we depend on outer conditions, whether people, experiences, countries, religions, wealth or fame, we are in constant fear of losing our footing, because everything changes and vanishes. The only way we can have real peace and happiness, is by being independent of all around us. That means gaining access to the purity of our mind without thinking, which involves staying on our meditation subject long enough for our consciousness to change. The thinking consciousness is the consciousness we all know. It contains constant ups and downs, either liking or disliking, wanting something in the future or regretting something about the past, hoping for better days or remembering worse ones. It is always anxious and cannot be expected to be totally peaceful.

We are familiar with a different consciousness also, for instance when we love someone very much. That emotion changes our consciousness to where we are only giving from the heart. We know a different consciousness when we are involved with religious activities, with faith and confidence aroused. We are giving ourselves to an ideal. None of that lasts through, and all depends upon outer conditions.

Through meditation we can change our consciousness to an awareness of purity within, which all of us have, only that it is obscured through thinking. At that time we realise that such an independent peace and happiness are only possible when the "me" and "mine" are forgotten for a moment, when "I want to be happy" is eliminated. It is impossible to have peace when thinking about "self." This will be our first inkling of what the Buddha meant, when he said non-self (*anattā*) is the way out of dukkha.

Because it is difficult for the mind to stay on the meditation subject, we have to use everything that arises for insight. Eventually the mind becomes clear and sharp and is no longer bothered by the outer manifestations that touch upon it, such as sound and thought, which are the most common ones. Finally a depth of concentration is reached.

When unpleasant feelings arise let us use them for insight. We didn't ask for the feelings, why are they ours? They are certainly changeable, they get worse or better, they move their position, and they give us a very good indication that the body is dukkha.

The body is not doing anything except sitting, and yet we have dukkha, for the simple reason of not liking the feeling as it is. When we use the unpleasant feeling to actually realise the first and second Noble Truths (*ariyasacca*), we've come nearer to the Dhamma in our hearts. The first Noble Truth is the Noble Truth of dukkha, the second is the reason for dukkha, namely craving. In this case, we are craving to get rid of the unpleasant feelings. If we were totally accepting of the feeling, not making any value judgments, there would be no dukkha.

We can try letting go of this craving for a moment; anyone with some strength of mind can do that. Just accepting the feeling as it is, not disliking it. Then there is no dukkha, for just that moment. That will be a profound insight experience, because it will show without the shadow of a doubt that if we drop our desires, dukkha disappears. Naturally when the body feels uncomfortable, it is difficult to drop the craving to get rid of that discomfort. But anybody can do it for just one moment, and it is an essential and in-depth experience of the Dhamma.

When we are able to step back to observe our thought processes, we realise that the mind is continually thinking. For someone who has not practised meditation previously it may take from five to ten minutes to become aware of that, but for an experienced meditator it may only take a second or two. Next we can see what kind of thinking we are indulging in and the more often we see it, the less enraptured we will be with it. We become aware of the fact that this is the way the human mind acts, not just ours, but everybody's, we will know the truth about the mind. There is nothing else to be seen except that. When we observe that the thinking goes on and that it is insignificant, it will be so much easier to let go. We also see how very fleeting thoughts are, how they come and go all the time. We will know from experience then, that no real happiness is to be found in something so short-lived, yet the whole world is trying to achieve happiness that way. We cannot even remember what we thought a moment ago, how can that bring happiness? Such insights make it possible to drop the distractions and get back to the meditation subject.

We are using the two approaches of calm and insight in conjunction with each other. When calm is firmly established, insight arises spontaneously. It is important to realise that calm meditation is essential. If the ocean has high waves and we want to look beneath the surface to see what can be found there, we cannot recognise anything at all while the waves are heaving. There is too much movement, all is stirred up and nothing is to be seen. When the waves subside and the ocean surface becomes calm and transparent, then we can look underneath the surface of the water and see sand, coral and multi-coloured fish. It is the same with the mind. When the mind has all the waves and motions of thinking, that churning makes it impossible to see absolute reality. On the contrary, the mind refuses to look beyond ordinary knowing. But when the mind becomes totally calm, then there is no value judgment, and we can see easily what lies underneath the surface.

In order to understand the Buddha's Teaching, we have to get below the surface, otherwise our insights will be superficial. The calm mind is the means for delving below relative reality. While we are trying to become calm, at the same time we are objectively examining all that arises, so that there is more and more support for letting go of the thinking. The less we believe in our thoughts, the less we expect of them and the happier we will be to let them go. Then we get an inkling of what inner peace and happiness mean.

These inner feelings are most pronounced in meditation, but can be carried into daily living in a milder form, primarily because the mind knows it can always return to peace and happiness in meditation, without having to depend on any situation or any person. Worldly affairs no longer have the former sting in them; they are just happening, that is all, the same as thinking and feeling are arising and ceasing, without an owner or a maker.

III. Awake and Aware

It is important to experience and not to believe. In order to do that, we have to pay attention. In the famous and often quoted Kālāma Sutta, the Buddha gives ten points which are not suitable as criteria to follow a teacher or a spiritual path. All of them have to do with a belief system because of traditional lineage or because of sacred books. Not to believe but to find out for ourselves is the often repeated injunction of the Buddha. Unless we do that, we cannot have an inner vision, which is the first step that takes us on to the noble path.

An inner vision is an understood experience. Without that, insight cannot arise. That holds true for small matters in daily life, just as it holds true for the deepest and most profound understanding of the Buddha's teaching. If for instance somebody is not pleased with us and we do not understand why, we shall have that same disharmony happen to us over and over again. We need to realise that we may have said or done something to cause that displeasure. This is a small matter showing the need for understanding an experience.

If we think these happenings are something outside of ourselves, we cannot change our attitudes. Practising Dhamma means to change ourselves constantly to reach out towards the sublime. If change were not possible, the Buddha would have given a lifetime of teaching in vain.

Unless we pay total attention to every detail we will never change towards the sublime. Attention to detail is the core of mindfulness. Most people lack the practice and also the instructions to be truly mindful. It is one thing to read about it, but an entirely different matter to do it. Mindfulness is the essence of understanding, because without it there is no seeing into the heart of any phenomena.

Watching the breath means "knowing exactly." Mindfulness is no judgmental, not discriminating, not telling stories. Mindfulness knows when there is concentration (*samādhi*) and when there is not, when the mind wanders off and when the mind becomes peaceful. Perfect mindfulness knows every moment that is occurring.

There are four foundations of mindfulness (*satipaṭṭhāna*): When we just know the body, its parts and its movements, without thinking, it is mindfulness of the body (*kāyānupassanā*). When we pay attention to our feelings and do not react to them but only observe, then we are using mindfulness of feeling (*vedanānupassanā*). When we know we are thinking, it is mindfulness of thought or mind (*cittānupassanā*) and when we know what the content of the thought is, it is mindfulness of mind objects (*dhammānupassanā*). If we are not paying attention, we are not really awake. We need to practise clear attention to all of these at all times.

It is possible for the mind to become concentrated during meditation. If there is a feeling of peacefulness, we have to know that quite clearly. Without realising what is happening, we cannot go further, because we do not know where we are at. This is an important detail of meditation: knowing exactly what's happening and being able to verbalise it after the occurrence. The verbalization is the understood experience, and occurs naturally after the experience. This holds true for any mind-state and for any feeling. The Dhamma is the Buddha's verbalised experience. Unless we can do that with our own experiences, we are left with a belief system which can dull the mind. But meditation is to sharpen the mind. The mindful mind is a sharpened axe, with a finely honed blade which can cut through all our illusions. When we sit in meditation, we can get to know the disturbances of our own mind: such as the dull mind that does not know what is going on, or the sleepy mind, the distracted or the resisting mind, that does not want to obey. That is mindfulness of mind objects.

Like most human beings, we have a distracted mind, geared so much towards trying to resist the unpleasant and crave the pleasant, that this pattern is very difficult to change. If we find ourselves resisting the unpleasant, seeking the pleasant, we just know that this is a normal habit pattern. This is how this little spaceship earth operates, and how our economy works. Do you know anybody who is blissfully happy because of it? It is an impossible venture, it is a guaranteed failure, yet everybody is still trying. We have all been trying long enough, we can give it up, at least for the time we are meditating. However it is possible to get rid of dukkha, but not by eliminating the unpleasant sensations, only by getting rid of our reaction to them. This is the most important primary entrance into the spiritual path. Unless this is perfectly understood, the rest will not fall into place. We won't get rid of the unpleasantness of sitting, or of mosquitoes, or of anything unpleasant we may encounter. All is mind-made and therefore mind-reacted. Dukkha disappears when our reactions disappear.

Unless we know that we are the creators of our own dukkha, the Dhamma remains a mystery. We start practising when we no longer blame our surroundings, other people, the political situation, the economy or the weather. We see only our own reactions. Naturally our reactions are not immediately going to be all favourable and wholesome. That will take a while. But at least we can start doing something about ourselves.

Mindfulness needs to be used not only in our meditation practice, but also every time we move, feel or think in our daily life. While awake, mindfulness has to be our primary objective. We have to come to terms with ourselves. Only then will the world make sense one day. The universe is this mind and body. We find out what this mind and body are all about, and we will know the universe and its underlying truth. All is distinctively the same, but we have to know what it is.

When we come out of meditation, we should be aware of opening our eyes, moving our body, of everything we are doing. Why? First of all, it will keep us from thinking unwholesome, negative thoughts. It facilitates meditation. The mind needs to be kept in check and not allowed to run wild. The ordinary, unpractised mind is like a wild bull running around in a garden. It can make a mess of the garden in no time. That is what our minds are doing. They are making an awful mess of this world we live in. We do not even have to read the newspapers to know about it. It is to be seen everywhere, and comes from our own minds. All of us are included, except the enlightened ones. A wild mind cannot meditate. It has to be caught, kept in check, and a halter put on. Every time it runs away, we bring it back with mindfulness, like training a wild horse which in its wild state cannot benefit anyone. If the horse is tamed and trained it can be extremely useful. How much more this is true of the mind!

Mindfulness of the body means that we know the movements of all parts. As we watch ourselves, we will see that there is mind and body. The mind giving the orders, the body following suit. We can recognise too that sometimes the body cannot obey because it is weak. This is our first entrance into insight, realising there are mind and body and the mind being the more important one. The difference between a trained and an untrained person is the understood experience.

Mindfulness of the body extends to the other aspects of mindfulness as well. If, for instance, we are thinking about the future we are no longer paying attention to the body; instead we can pay attention to the thought process. We know that we are thinking, and are making kamma. The thoughts are the mental formations (saṅkhāra), as well as the kamma formations. We are the owners of our kamma. Whatever we think, that we will be. It is an impersonal process which has nothing to do with any particular entity.

Then we can become aware of the content of our thoughts, which means knowing whether it is wholesome or not. We can learn to drop any negative thinking and replace it. This is where our meditation training comes in, which is not divorced from outer activities. When we pay attention to the breath in meditation and a thought intervenes, we learn to let go of the thought and come back to the breath. The same procedure is used in daily life to let go of unwholesome thoughts. We substitute at that time with a wholesome thought, just as we substitute with the breath in meditation.

Mindfulness of the thinking process is what the Buddha called the "four supreme efforts."[2] They constitute the heart of the purification process. The spiritual path is the path of purification and hinges on mindfulness. In the Satipaṭṭhāna Sutta the Buddha said: "There is only one way for the purification of beings, for the overcoming of dukkha, for the final elimination of pain, grief and lamentation, for entering the noble path, for realising Nibbāna, that is mindfulness." To practise the purification process is necessary not only for our own peace of mind, for adding to the peace in the world, but also in order to be able to meditate.

The hope that we might sit down on a cushion, watch the breath and become concentrated is an illusion. We have to have the mind in proper shape for it. Therefore, we must practise these four supreme efforts not only while we are meditating, but in everyday life. We will gain inner peace which everybody is looking for and very few people ever find.

---

2. The four supreme efforts (*padhāna*) are: 1. To avoid unwholesome states of mind; 2. To overcome unwholesome states of mind; 3. To develop wholesome states of mind; 4. To maintain wholesome states of mind.

The first effort is not to let an unwholesome thought arise which has not yet arisen. This requires sharp mindfulness. A thought which has not yet arisen creates waves ahead of it. To realise that these waves are foreboding no good, needs much attention and practice. The second effort, not to continue an unwholesome thought which has already arisen, can be done by anyone of good will, if it is understood that there is nobody else to blame. Unwholesome thinking is not due to outer triggers, but results strictly from our own defilements.

The third step is to make a wholesome thought arise which has not yet arisen. This means that we continually watch over our mind and encourage positive, wholesome thoughts where none are present even under the most trying circumstances.

Finally, to make a wholesome thought, which has already arisen, continue. In the meditation practice, this concerns our meditation subject. But in daily life it means our mind's reaction. If we have some sensitivity towards ourselves, we can feel that there is a disturbance within when unwholesome thinking arises, a feeling of resistance. Unwholesome thoughts have been thought of so often for so many years, that they have become part and parcel of our thinking process. It takes mindfulness and determination to let go.

In meditation we become aware that our unwholesome thoughts are not caused by someone or something external. Then we gain the power of mind to drop what we do not want, to keep and substitute with what is useful for us. These four supreme efforts are the fourth foundation of mindfulness, which is concerned with the contents of our thoughts. If everybody in the world were practising this, it would be a better world to live in.

Our inner being manifests in feeling, which arises through our sense contacts. Thinking is also a sense contact. Unwholesome thinking produces unpleasant feelings, such as being ill at ease, or unhappy. Seeing, hearing, tasting, touching, smelling are the five outer senses. Thinking is the inner one. All of them make contact and produce a feeling. There is the eye and the eye object. When both are in good condition, the eye consciousness arises and seeing results. The sense base, the sense object and the sense consciousness meet. When we know how this being, which we call "me," operates, we can stop the pre-programmed print-out that is always answering the same way. It is quite possible to predict how a person will react to any given stimulus, because we have a programme which has never been interrupted yet. To discontinue it, we first have to know that there is a programme and what it consists of.

For instance, we have the hearing base, which is the ear drum; then there is sound. When the hearing consciousness arises, because both base and object are present, hearing results and from that a feeling arises. The ear can only hear sound, the eye can only see form and colour. The mind does all the explaining. Everybody has a slightly different explanation, so that nobody sees or hears anything alike. When one man sees a woman, and sees her form and colour, the mind says "Is not she beautiful, I must marry her." When I see that same woman, I do not think anything like that.

Yet everyone tries to convince the people around them that what they themselves are seeing and hearing is correct. Because they often cannot convince others, they start shooting or persecuting them.

Thinking is also a sense contact. There is the brain base and there are ideas. The mind consciousness arises, contacting the idea and thinking starts. From that a feeling results. If we think we love every being, whether we actually can do it or not, we certainly get a warm pleasant feeling from the thought. By the same token, if we think we hate a person, we get a cold and distant feeling. Now, here comes the reaction to the feeling, which is either wanting/craving or not wanting/rejecting. By being attentive to ourselves, we can experience that quite clearly. The reaction to the feeling is our renewed entry into duality and dukkha. At the same time it provides us with the doorway out of all difficulties. If for once we do not react, but know a feeling just as a feeling, if we can do that, mindfulness has been established. We also gain the confidence that we can do it again and are actually practising spiritual purification. That is an important inner conviction. The Buddha said we need both, study and practice. Study helps us to know something of what the Buddha taught, but if we do not practise, then we are only parrots or hypocrites, proclaiming something we have no personal experience with.

Through our practice of mindfulness we become aware of the feelings which arise when we make sense contacts. Feelings happen all the time and need to be recognised so that we can change our instinctive way of living to a deliberate way of being alive. Instinctively we are a constant reactor; deliberately we become an actor.

Probably the most important lesson we can learn is to keep our mindfulness going in our every-day activities. We can practise wherever we are, at home, in the market, in the office, writing letters, telephoning, any time at all. The meditation itself gives us the impetus, showing how awareness removes the obstacles inherent in our viewpoints. We cannot see the whole, only parts. We see what is around us, but we never see beyond that. With mindfulness comes an opening, where everything seems to fall into place and has an interconnection. We lose our exaggerated sense of self-importance, and can unite more with all manifestations. All these are still side issues. Mindfulness means knowing. As we know and really experience, we can prove, eventually, the Four Noble Truths to ourselves. Then our work is completed.

Mindfulness has, as one of its factors, the ability to be one-pointed. We do not become foggy or distracted, but can keep the mind in its place. We have to realise that the mind's obstructions are a human calamity and not a personal one. This understanding helps us to patiently endure and gradually change.

IV. Supreme Efforts

We can notice fairly easily what our mind does. It reflects and reacts and it often has fantasies and also moods. Anyone who does not meditate will believe in all of that. Even those who do meditate might still believe in the reactions of their own mind to the outer stimuli, or might believe the moods which come into the mind are to be taken seriously, that whatever the mind is doing is due to an outside occurrence and not to an inner reaction. This is easily seen if we watch our thinking process not only in meditation but in daily living.

The Buddha gave very exact instructions how to counteract any unskilful mind states and produce skilful ones. They can briefly be expressed as "avoiding," "overcoming," "developing," and "maintaining," and are called "the four supreme efforts," which have been briefly mentioned before. They are part of the thirty-seven factors of enlightenment, so must be part of our practice. When perfected, they are part of the enlightenment process.

You may have heard the expression "Nibbāna and saṃsāra are both in the same place." It is not a true saying, because there is no such "place." How can Nibbāna, liberation, emancipation, enlightenment, and samsara, the round of birth and death, be together? In a way they can, because they are both in the mind, in everybody's mind. Except that everyone is only aware of one of them, namely that which makes us continue in the round of birth and death; not only when this body disappears and it is called "death" or when a body reappears and it is called "birth." But there is constant birth and death in our every moment of existence. There is the birth of skilful and unskilful thoughts and the dying away of them. There is the birth of feelings, pleasant, unpleasant or neutral, and the dying away of them. There is the birth of the arising of this body and its dying away moment after moment, except that we are not mindful enough to become aware of that.

We can see this quite clearly when we look at a photo of ourselves taken ten or twenty years ago. We look entirely different from what we see in the mirror now. But it does not follow that a body takes a leap of twenty years and then changes itself suddenly. It has changed moment by moment until after a longer time-span, it is finally noticeable to us. With more mindfulness we could have known it all along, because there is constant birth and death in the body, the same as with thoughts and feelings. This is samsara, the round of birth and death within us, due to our craving to keep or renew what we think is "me." When there is liberation, that craving ceases, whatever dies is left to die.

Although we have the potential for liberation, our awareness is not able to reach it, because we are concerned with what we already know. We are habit-formed and habit-prone and every meditator becomes aware of the mind habits with their old and tried reactions to outside triggers. They have not necessarily been useful in the past, but they are still repeated out of habit. The same applies to our moods, which are arising and passing away and have no other significance than a cloud has in the sky, which only denotes the kind of weather there is, without any universal truth in that. Our moods only denote the kind of weather our mind is fabricating, if it believes in the mood.

The four supreme efforts are, in the first place, the avoiding of unwholesome, unskilful thought processes. If we look at them as unskilful, we can accept the fact of learning a new skill more easily. Avoiding means we do not let certain thoughts arise, neither reactions to moods, nor to outside triggers. If we find ourselves habitually reacting in the same way to the same kind of situation, we may be forced to avoid such situations, so that we can finally gain the insight which needs to be culled from it. While we are reacting to a situation or mood, we cannot assess it dispassionately, because our reactions overpower the mind.

Avoiding, in a Dhamma sense, means to avoid the unskilful thought; in a practical sense we may have to avoid whatever arouses such mind states in us. That, however, must not go to the length of running away as the slightest provocation, which is a well known, yet unsuccessful method of getting out of unpleasant reactions. Habitually running away from situations, which create unwholesome reactions in us, will not bring about a peaceful mind. Only if there is one particular trigger, which arouses unskilful responses in us over and over again, we may have to move away from it without blaming anyone. We just realise that we have not yet been able to master ourselves under certain circumstances. Just as we do not blame the unpleasant feeling anywhere in the body, but realise that we haven't mastered our non-reaction to dukkha yet, and therefore must change our posture.

It amounts to exactly the same thing. One is a physical move, the other is a mental one. All it means is that we haven't quite mastered a particular situation yet. It brings us to the realisation that there is still more to be learned about ourselves. Blaming anything outside of ourselves is useless; it only aggravates the situation and adds more unwholesome thinking to it.

In order to avoid unskilful reactions in the mind, we have to be attentive and know the way our mind works before we verbalise. We can learn about that in meditation. Awareness is the prime mover in meditation. It is not viable or useful to have calm and peaceful mind states without being completely aware of how we attained them, remained in them and came out of them. Having learned this through our meditative practice, enables us to realise how our mind works in daily life, for example, before it says anything, such as: "I cannot stand this situation" or "I hate this person." When that happens, an unwholesome state has already been established.

Before the mind is allowed to fall into this trap, a dense and unpleasant feeling can be noticed, which acts as a warning that an unwholesome mind state is approaching, which can be dropped before it has even established itself. It is much easier to let go before the negativity has taken hold but it is harder to recognise. When we notice that a mind state is approaching which does not seem to be accompanied by peace and happiness, we can be sure it will be unwholesome. The more we train ourselves to be mindful of our mind states, the more we realise the unhappiness we cause ourselves and others through unskilful thinking.

When we have not been able to avoid an unwholesome mind, we have to practise to overcome it. Because of the difficulty of becoming aware in time to avoid negativities, we have to be very clear on how to overcome them. Dropping a thought is an action and not a passive reaction, yet it is difficult to do, because the mind needs something to grasp. In meditation we need a subject, such as the breath or the feelings or sensations to hold onto, before the mind can become calm and peaceful. When we want to overcome unskilful mind states, it is easier to substitute with wholesome thinking, than just trying to let go of unwholesomeness.

If we entertain the negative mind states for any length of time, they become more and more at home. As they make themselves comfortable, we are more and more inclined to believe them and finally come out with thoughts such as "I always hate people who do not agree with me" or "I always get nervous about thunder." These statements are designed to show our own unchanging character, giving our ego an extra boost. The only reason these states might have become ingrained in our character is that having entertained negativities for so long, we can no longer imagine being without them. Yet these are nothing but unskilful mind states, which can and need to be changed. The quicker we substitute, the better it is for our own peace of mind.

If we have dislike or rejection concerning a person, we may remember something good about that person and be able to substitute the negative thought with something concretely positive. Everyone is endowed with both qualities, good and evil, and if we pick on the negative, then we will constantly be confronted with that aspect, rather than the opposite. With some people this will be more difficult that with others. They are our tests, so to say. Nobody gets away in this life without such tests. Life is an adult education class with frequent examinations, which are being thrown at us at any time. We are not told in advance what is in store for us so we should be prepared all the time.

As we learn the skill of substitution and do it successfully once, we gain confidence in our own ability. There is no reason when why we cannot repeat this whenever needed. The relief we feel is all the incentive we need for practice.

When we are confronted with situations which we find difficult to handle, we can remember that we are faced with a learning experience. Overcoming unwholesome mind states needs mind power, which we develop through our meditation practice. If we are not yet able to keep our attention in meditation where we want it to be, we will not be able yet to change our mind when we want to do so. The more skill we develop in meditation, the easier it will be for us to either "avoid" or "overcome." By the same token, as we practise substitution in daily living, we assist our meditation. When we realise that our mind is not a solid entity which has to react in certain ways, but is a movable, changeable phenomenon, which can be clear and illuminated, then we will more and more try to protect it from unwholesomeness. It is often a revelation to a new meditator to find out that the mind is not a fixed and believable reactor but can be influenced and changed at will.

The way to develop wholesome states of mind is to try to cultivate these when they have not arisen yet. If the mind is neutrally engaged or has a tendency to weigh, judge and criticise, feel hurt or be ego-centred, we deliberately counteract these tendencies to develop skilful mind states. We acknowledge that all negative states are not conducive to our own happiness, peace and harmony. When we develop loving-kindness, compassion, sympathetic joy and equanimity, we experience that these states are conducive to our own inner well-being. Obviously we will then try again and again to cultivate the mind states which result in personal contentment. To develop wholesome states of mind because we understand they are good for us is a powerful insight. When our mind is at peace, we realise that, while there are innumerable unwholesome situations in the world, our dukkha is doubled if we have an unwholesome reaction to them. . It will neither relieve the situation, nor be helpful to anyone.

If we develop a capacity for seeing the positive and using whatever arises as a learning situation, trying to keep in mind the four supreme emotions mentioned above, then there remains only the last effort, namely to maintain skilful mind states. Not having reached full liberation from all underlying tendencies (*anusaya*), we will not be able to maintain positive states at all times, but our mindfulness can be sharp enough to tell us when we are not succeeding. That is the awareness we need to effect changes. When we are not able to maintain wholesomeness, we can always try again. Should we start blaming ourselves or others, however, we are adding a second negative state of mind and are blocking our progress.

A skill can be learned; we have all learned many skills in this life. This is the sort of ability well worth cultivating, more important than proficiencies. This is not a character trait we either possess or lack. Everybody's mind is capable of developing the wholesome and letting go of the unwholesome. But that also does not mean that we find everything wonderful and beautiful from now on. That too is not realistic. When there is unwholesomeness within and without, dislike to it is not an effective reaction to bring peace and happiness. What can be practised though is equanimity. The pinnacle of all emotional states is equanimity, even-mindedness, which is developed through our meditation practice and based on insight. Equanimity is our tool in daily living to develop and maintain wholesome mind states.

It is neither useful to suppress nor to pretend by thinking "I ought to be" or "I should be." Only awareness of what is happening in our mind and learning the skill of changing our mind is called for. Eventually our mind will be a finely tuned instrument, the only one in the whole of the universe that can liberate us from all dukkha. All of us have that instrument and the guidelines of the Buddha teach us the skill to use this instrument to the best advantage; not to believe its moods and reactions to outer stimuli, but to watch and protect it and realise its potential for complete liberation.

If we want a good tool, we need to look after it in the best possible manner. This means not letting any dirt particles accumulate, but to clean it up as quickly as possible. The same criterion applies to our mind. This is probably the hardest skill to learn, which is the reason so few people do it, but a meditator is on the right path towards just that, by realising that the mind cannot be believed implicitly, being much too fanciful and fleeting.

The four supreme efforts are called "supreme," not only because they are supremely difficult, but also supremely beneficial. A serious meditator wants to transcend the human realm while still in human form and these efforts are our challenge. They are so well explained by the Buddha that we can clearly see the difficulties we are faced with and the reasons why we are still roaming about in samsara. But we do not have to continue that unendingly. Knowing the path and the way to tread upon it, we have the opportunity to become free of all fetters.

V. Expanded Consciousness

Just as we are capable of changing the body at will, the same applies to the mind. Changing the body can occur when we eat less and get thin, eat more and get fat, drink too much alcohol and spoil our liver, smoke too much and sicken our lungs. We can exercise to get muscles, or train to run fast or jump high, or to become very proficient at tennis or cricket. The trained body is able to do many things which ordinary people usually cannot do because they haven't trained for it. We know, for example, of people who can jump two or three times further than is common, or run ten times faster than anyone else. We may have seen people doing stunts with their bodies which look miraculous, or people who can use their minds in seemingly miraculous ways, but these "miracles" are really just due to training.

Meditation is the only training there is for the mind. Physical training is usually connected with physical discipline. The mind needs mental discipline, practice in meditation.

We can change our mind from unwholesome to wholesome thinking. Just like a person who wants to be an athlete has to start at the beginning of body training, the same needs to be done for mind training. First we cope with the ordinary, later with the extraordinary. The recollection of our own death brings us the realisation that all that is happening will be finished very soon, because all of us are going to die. Even though we may not know the exact date, it is guaranteed to happen. With the death contemplation in mind, it does not matter so much any more what goes on around us, since all is only important for a very limited time.

We may be able to see that only our kamma-making matters, doing the best we can every single day, every single moment. Helping others takes pride of place. There is no substitute for that. Someone else can benefit from our skills and possessions since we cannot keep them and cannot take them with us. We might as well give all away as quickly as possible.

One of the laws of the universe is the more one gives away, the more one gets. Nobody believes it, that is why everyone is trying to make more money and own more things, yet it is a law of cause and effect. If we would believe it and act accordingly we would soon find out. However it will only be effective if the giving is done in purity. We can give our time, our caring and our concern for others' well-being. We have the immediate benefit of happiness in our own heart, when we see the joy we have given to someone else. This is about the only satisfaction we can expect in this life which is of a nature that does not disappear quickly, because we can recollect the deed and our own happiness.

If we really believe in our impending death, not just use the words, our attitude towards people and situations changes completely. We are no longer the same person then. The person we have been until now has not brought us complete satisfaction, contentment and peacefulness. We might as well become a different person, with a new outlook. We no longer try to make anything last, because we know the temporary nature of our involvement. Consequently nothing has the same significance anymore.

It could be compared to inviting people to our home for a meal. We are worried and anxious whether the food will taste just right, whether all the comforts are there and nothing missing. The house should be immaculate for the guests. While they are visiting we are extremely concerned that they are getting everything they could possibly want. Afterwards we are concerned whether they like it at our house, have been happy there and whether they are going to tell other friends that it was a pleasant visit. These are our attitudes because we own the place. If we are a guest we do not care what food is being served, because that is up to the hostess. We do not worry whether everything is in apple-pie order because it is not our house.

This body is not our house, no matter how long we live. It is a temporary arrangement of no significance. Nothing belongs to us, we are guests here. Maybe we will be present for another week or year, or ten or twenty years. But being a guest, what can it matter how everything works? The only thing we can do when we are guests in someone's house is to try to be pleasant and helpful to our hosts. All else is totally insignificant, otherwise our consciousness will remain in the marketplace.

Does it not only matter to elevate our consciousness and awareness to where we can see beyond our immediate concerns? There is always the same thing going on: getting up, eating breakfast, washing, dressing, thinking and planning, cooking, buying things, talking to people, going to work, going to bed, getting up … over and over again. Is that enough for a lifetime? All of us are trying to find something within that daily grind which will give us joy. But nothing lasts and moreover all are connected with reaching out to get something. If we were to remember each morning that death is certain, but now have another day to live, gratitude and determination can arise to do something useful with that day. A second recollection would be to remember how to change our mind from enmity, harm and unhappiness to their opposites.

Repeated remembering makes it possible to change the mind gradually. The body does not change overnight to become athletic and neither does the mind change instantly. But if we do not continually train it, it is just going to stay the same it has always been, which is not conductive to a harmonious and peaceful life. Most people find a lot of unpleasantness, anxiety and fear in their lives. Fear is a human condition, based on our ego delusion. We are afraid that our ego will be destroyed and annihilated.

This willingness to change our mind should make it possible to live each day meaningfully, which is the difference between just being alive and living. We would do at least one thing each day, which either entails spiritual growth for ourselves or helpfulness and consideration for others, preferably both. If we add one meaningful day to the next, we wind up with a meaningful life. Otherwise we have an egocentric life, which can never be satisfying. If we forget about our own desires and rejections and are just concerned with spiritual growth and eventual emancipation and with being helpful to other people, then our dukkha is greatly reduced. It reaches a point where it is only the underlying movement in all of existence and no longer personal suffering and unhappiness. As long as we suffer and are unhappy, our lives are not very useful. Having grief, pain and lamentation does not mean we are very sensitive, but rather that we haven't been able to find a solution.

We spend hours and hours, buying food, preparing it, eating it, washing up afterwards, and thinking about the next meal. Twenty minutes of recollection on how we should live should not be taxing our time. Naturally, we can also spend much more time on such contemplations which are a way to give the mind a new direction. Without training, the mind is heavy and not very skilful, but when we give the mind a new direction, then we learn to protect our own happiness. This is not connected with getting what we want and getting rid of what we do not want. It is a skill of the mind to realise what is helpful and produces happiness.

This new direction which arises from contemplation can be put into action. What can we actually do? We have all heard far too many words which sound right, but words alone won't accomplish anything. There has to be an underlying realisation that these words require mental or physical action. The Buddha mentioned that if we hear a Dhamma discourse and have confidence in its truth, first we must remember the words. Then we can see whether we are able to do what is required of us.

If we wish to be free of enmity, we can recollect such a determination again and again. Now comes the next step: How can we actualize that? When going about our daily life we have to be very attentive whether any enmity is arising, and if so, to substitute with love and compassion. That is the training of the mind. The mind does not feel so burdened then, so bogged down in its own pre-determined course because we realise change is possible. When the mind feels lighter and clearer, it can expand. Activating the teachings of the Buddha changes the awareness of the mind, so that the everyday, ordinary activities are no longer so significant. They are seen to be necessary to keep the body alive and the mind interested in the manifold proliferations (*papañca*) that exist in the world.

The realisation arises that if we have been able to change our mind even that much, there may be more to the universe than we have ever been able to touch upon with the ordinary mind. The determination may come to make the mind extraordinary. Just as in an athlete, enormous feats of balance, discipline and strength of the body are possible, just so it is feasible for the mind. The Buddha talked about expanded awareness as a result of proper concentration, time and time again. Right concentration means a change of consciousness because we are then not connected to the usual, relative knowing.

Being able to change our mind's direction, we are no longer so enmeshed in the ordinary affairs, but know that there must be more. Through having been disciplined, strengthened and balanced, a mind can perform feats of mental awareness which seem quite extraordinary but are just a result of training. It means getting out of the mental rut. If we have a wet driveway and drive a truck over it time and time again, the ruts get deeper and deeper and in the end the truck may be stuck fast. Such are our habitual responses that we have in our everyday affairs. Practising meditation lifts us out of those ruts because the mind gets a new dimension. Contemplation and resulting action make a new pathway in our lives, where the old ruts are left behind. The ruts are a constant reaction to our sense stimuli, of hearing, seeing, smelling, tasting, touching and thinking. It is a great pity to use a good human life just to be a reactor. It is much more useful and helpful to become an actor, which means deliberate thinking, saying and doing.

It is possible to eventually have the kind of concentration where the meditation subject is no longer needed. The meditation subject is nothing but a key, or we can also call it a hook to hang the mind on, so that it will not attend to worldly affairs. When concentration has arisen, it can be likened to the key having finally found the keyhole and the door being unlocked. When we unlock the door of true concentration (*samādhi*) we find a house with eight rooms, which are the eight meditative absorptions *(jhānas)*. Having been able to enter the first room, there is no reason why, with practice, determination and diligence, we cannot gradually enter into all of them. Here the mind actually lets go of the thinking process as we know it and reverts to a state of experiencing.

The first thing that happens when concentration has arisen is a sense of well being. Unfortunately there is a mistaken view prevalent that the meditative absorptions are neither possible nor necessary. This view is contrary to the Buddha's teaching. Any instructions he has ever given for the pathway to liberation always included the meditative absorptions. They are right concentration (*sammāsamādhi*), the eighth step on the Noble Eightfold Path. It is also incorrect to believe that it is no longer possible to attain true concentration; many people do so without even realising it and need support and direction to further their efforts. Meditation needs to include the meditative absorptions because they are the expansion of consciousness or awareness and provide access to a totally different universe than we have ever realised.

The mental states that arise through the meditative absorptions make it possible to live our daily life with a sense of what is significant and what is not. Having seen, for instance, that it is possible to grow large trees, we no longer believe that trees are always small, even though the trees in our own backyard may be tiny because the soil is poor. If we have seen large trees, we know that they exist, and we may even try to find a place where they grow. The same applies to our mental states. Having seen the possibility of expanded consciousness, we no longer believe that ordinary consciousness is all there is, or that the breath is all there is to meditation.

The breath is the hook on which we hang the mind so that we can open the door to true meditation. Having opened the door, we experience physical well-being, manifested in many different ways. It may be a strong or a mild sensation, but it is always connected with a pleasant feeling. Of that pleasure the Buddha said: "This is a pleasure that is not to be feared" (Mahāsaccakasutta). Unless we experience the joy of the meditative absorptions, a joy independent of the world, we will never resign from the world, but will continue to see the world as our home. Only when we realize that the joy in the meditative absorptions is independent of all worldly conditions, will we finally be able to say, "The world and its manifold attractions are not interesting any more" so that dispassion will set in. If we has nothing else, why should we resign from that which occasionally does give pleasure and joy? How can we do that? It is impossible to let go of all the joys and pleasures which the world offers if we have nothing to replace them. This is the first reason why in the Buddha's teaching the meditative absorptions are of the essence. We cannot let go when we are still under the impression that with this body and these senses we can get what we are looking for, namely happiness.

The Buddha encourages us to look for happiness, but we need to look in the right place. He said we would be able to protect our own happiness. Even the very first instance of gaining physical pleasure in meditation already illuminates the fact that something inside us gives joy and happiness. The physical well-being also arouses pleasurable interest which helps to keep us on the meditation cushion. Although it is a physical sensation, it is not the same sort of feeling that we are familiar with. It is different because it has arisen from a different source. Ordinary pleasant physical feelings come from touch contact. This one comes from concentration. Obviously, having different causes, they must also be different in their results. Touch is gross, concentration is subtle. Therefore the meditative feeling has a more subtle spiritual quality than the pleasant feeling we can get through touch. Knowing clearly that the only condition necessary for happiness is concentration, we will refrain from our usual pursuits of seeking pleasant people, tasty food, better weather, more wealth and not squander our mental energy on those. This is, therefore, a necessary first step towards emancipation.

We are now entering mind states that go beyond the everyday, worldly affairs... We all know the mind that is connected with ordinary matters. Such a mind worries about all sorts of things, is anxious, has plans, memories, hopes, dreams, likes, dislikes and reactions. It is a very busy mind. For the first time we may become acquainted with a mind which does not contain all these aspects. Pleasurable well-being has no thinking attached to it, it is an experience. Here we finally realise that the kind of thinking we are aware of will not give us the results we had hoped for. It is just good enough to project a willingness to meditate. We learn, even from that very first step, that the world cannot do for us what concentration can do. Happiness independent of outer conditions is far more satisfying than anything to be found in the world. We are also shown that the mind has the ability to expand into a different consciousness with which we had no previous contact, so that we gain first-hand experience of the fact that meditation is the means for spiritual emancipation.

Because of having had this pleasurable feeling, an inner joy arises. This gives the meditator the assurance that the pathway towards "non-self" is a pathway of joy and not of dukkha. Thereby the natural resistance to "non-self" is greatly lessened. Most people resist the idea that they are "nobody," even after they have understood it intellectually. But being able to experience these first two aspects of meditation, gives a clear indication that this is only possible when the "self," which is always thinking, is temporarily buried. Because when the self is active, it immediately says "Oh, is not that nice," and the concentration is finished. It has to be and experience where nothing says "I am experiencing." The explanation and understanding of what we have experienced comes later.

This is a clear realisation that, without "self," the inner joy is a much greater and more profound nature than any happiness we have known in this life. Therefore the determination to really come to grips with the Buddha's teachings will come to fruition. Until then, most people pick out a few aspects of the Dhamma, which they've heard about, and think that is sufficient. It may be devotion, chanting, festivals, doing good works, moral behaviour, all of which is fine, but the reality of the teaching is a great mosaic in which all these different pieces fall together into one huge, all encompassing whole. And the central core is "non-self" (anattā). If we use only a few of these mosaic pieces we will never get the whole picture. But being able to meditate makes a great deal of difference in our approach to that whole conglomerate of teaching, which encompasses body and mind and completely changes the person who practises like that.

We have to base our meditative ability on our daily practice. We cannot hope to sit down and meditate successfully, if all we can think about are worldly affairs, and if we do not try to reduce anger, envy, jealousy, pride, greed, hate, rejection in daily life. If we use mindfulness, clear comprehension and a calming of sensual desires, we have a foundation for meditation. As we practise in everyday affairs in conjunction with meditation, we see a slow and gradual change, as if an athlete has been training. The mind becomes strong and attends to the important issues in life. It does not get thrown about by everything that happens.

If we can give some time for contemplation and meditation each day and not forget mindfulness, we have a very good beginning for an expansion of consciousness. Eventually the universe looks quite different, based on our changed viewpoint. There is a Zen saying: "First the mountain is a mountain, then the mountain is no longer a mountain and in the end, the mountain is a mountain again." First we see everything in its relative reality; every person is a different individual, every tree is a particular kind, everything has some significance to our own lives. . Then we start practicing, and suddenly we see a different reality, which is universal and expansive. We become very involved with our own meditation and do not pay much attention to what is going on around us. We see an expansion and elevation of our consciousness; we know that our everyday reactions are not important. For a while, we may pay attention to just that and to living in a different reality. In the end, we come right back to where we were, doing all the same things as before, but no longer being touched by them. A mountain is just a mountain again. Everything returns to the same ordinary aspect it used to have, except it is no longer significant or separate.

The Discourse on Blessings (Mangala Sutta) describes the Arahant as: "… although touched by worldly circumstances, never his mind is wavering." The Enlightened One is touched by worldly circumstances, he acts like everybody else, he eats, sleeps, washes and talks to people but his mind does not waver. The mind stays cool and peaceful at all times.

VI. Kamma is Intention

I f we want to understand kamma and rebirth correctly we have to see them in the light of the characteristic of non-self (*anattā*). Some people proclaim non-self quite vividly and yet do not take it into consideration at all when they talk about "my" kamma and "my" rebirth. Especially "my" rebirth is absurd. Do they mean the last rebirth or future rebirth? Do we think it will be "me" again? In ordinary language we have little choice, yet the spoken word has evolved out of our thinking processes.

People often ask what is reborn if it is not "me"? Kamma as a residual effect in the rebirth-consciousness is reborn, but it certainly does not look or act like the one we know, does not have the same name, may not have the same form or sex, may not even be human. It has no other connection than kamma. Since we can see quite clearly that the one who is reborn only connects through kamma in the rebirth consciousness with a previous life, we can see just as clearly that kamma is impersonal, without identity. While we talk about "my" kamma, it is really an impersonal process. It is not crime and punishment although it may appear like that but this is one of the most commonly held views. Many of our entrenched views are so deeply ingrained that it becomes extremely difficult to understand anything radically different.

Kamma, actually, just means "action" and in the India of the Buddha that is how it was understood. In order to make people aware of what it really implies, the Buddha said: "Kamma, monks, I declare, is intention." Intention arises first in our thoughts and then generates speech and action. This was the new interpretation that the Buddha gave to kamma, because it was largely misunderstood and used as predetermined destiny. There were teachers in his day that taught it that way, which was denounced by the Buddha as wrong view (*micchādiṭṭhi*), misleading and liable to have unwholesome results. This view of pre-determined destiny is just as rampant today as it was at the Buddha's time. It is often voiced like this: "There is nothing I can do about it, it is my kamma." This is the greatest folly to which one can adhere because it puts the onus of one's own intentions on some nebulous previous person whom one does not even know. In other words, one does not take responsibility for one's own actions, which is a very common failing.

It is harder to find a person who does take responsibility than to find one who does not. Most people do not want to take responsibility for themselves, if they can just manage to stay alive. From that difficulty arises the idea of pre-determined destiny. "What can I do, it is not my fault, it is my kamma." That takes away all possibility for practising the Dhamma. The Buddha said: "If that were so, the holy life would not be possible, nor would it be feasible to become enlightened." This is the first wrong view that one has to quickly eliminate from one's thinking process, if one wants to practise a spiritual discipline.

Kamma is intention, and intention is now, which means kamma is being made now, in every waking moment. However when two people make the same kamma, they do not get the same results. This is another point the Buddha emphasised. Since kamma is impersonal, it is strictly concerned with a flow of events which are creating results by themselves. It is a matter of cause and effect. That is all there is, and the Buddha's teaching is sometimes called the teaching of cause and effect.

Sometimes we see people who are very nice, they would not hurt a fly, and yet a lot of misfortune befalls them. Or others who are difficult and unfriendly, but everything always seems to go right for them. How is this possible? It depends entirely upon their accumulations of good or bad kamma that have resulted in their particular mind continuum. The Buddha gave the following simile: "If one puts a teaspoon of salt in a cup of water, that cup becomes undrinkable. If one puts a teaspoon of salt in the Ganges River, it does not make the slightest difference to the river, the water remains exactly the same." If one makes bad kamma and has only a cupful of good kamma; the results will be disastrous. If one has a river full of good kamma to support one, the results will be negligible. Therefore, we can never compare the results that people have, because we do not know their past histories.

The residual mind continuum that we bring with us certainly has a bearing on this life, particularly on where we are born, under what circumstances and in what sort of family. The Buddha gave a simile for that: "If there is a herd of cows locked in a barn, and the barn door is opened, the cow that is the strongest will go out first. If there is not one like that, then the one who is the habitual leader will go out first; if there is no habitual leader then the one nearest the door will go out first. If there is none like that, they will all try to go out at the same time" This depicts the mind moments at death. Since death is imminent for everyone no matter what their age, it is skilful to be ready for it now.

The last thought-moment at death is the one that impels the rebirth consciousness to its next destination. We can compare that to going to sleep at night and our last thought-moment is that we will wake up at four o'clock in the morning. Most people can easily do that. The last thought-moment becomes the first one upon waking. Dying is exactly the same, except that the body that wakes up is a new one and looks different. It is likely that it will be a human being again, unless one has behaved too badly for such a rebirth. Even though people often wish for rebirth in a deva realm, most people probably return as human beings.

The last thought-moment is the one that connects with the strongest experience in this life time. If, for instance, one has murdered a person, that would be a very strong memory and could be the last thought-moment. If one has built a monastery or temple that may be a very strong thought formation (saṅkhāra). Or, if one has always kept one's moral conduct intact, that may be the last thought-moment. Whatever is the strongest in one's mind, that is most likely to arise.

Otherwise one's habitual thinking takes over. If one has usually been dissatisfied or angry, then that will be in the mind. If one has had much loving-kindness, compassion and helpfulness toward others, those thoughts will arise.

If there is no particular thinking habit, then that which comes nearest the sense doors at death takes precedence. The last sense to go is hearing. It is very common, therefore, in most religions that some devotional words are chanted by monks or priests which may help to have a good last thought-moment. If these last mental formations are wholesome, one's rebirth will be favourable. That does not mean that the rest of the kamma resultants disappear. It only means that the impulsion that arises at death takes a certain direction; therefore the last thought-moments are of crucial importance.

If one has been a very generous person, the recollection of one' generosity can be a last thought. It is therefore considered extremely beneficial to remind a dying person of all the good things they have done in this life, such as their generosity and their kindness, because ordinary worldlings (*puthujjana*) are apt to have regrets and self-blame. It has in recent years been recognised that dying is a very important part of living, even though in the West many people do not believe in rebirth. Everyone pays a lot of attention to the moment a baby is born, because that baby is going to be around for a long time, and will be an important member of the family. Few pay sufficient attention to the moment of death, because after all that person is gone, finished but it is now understood that this is not a wholesome way of treating a human being. In the West there are many hospitals for terminally ill and dying people, where great attention is paid to their mind states, to reduce or eliminate fear and anxiety. Yet, hardly anyone there believes in rebirth, but even without that, death is considered very important.

Another factor has entered into our death experience. We are now so technologically advanced that in some instances people who were clinically dead have been brought back to life in modern hospitals. A number of these people talked to their doctors about their "death" experiences. Some doctors, particularly Dr. Moody, wrote about these phenomena. An outstanding feature of the stories told is the fact that they were practically identical in their important aspects. This gives us another clue to non-self or corelessness *(anattā)*. All of them, without fail, were extremely pleased with their "death" and reluctant to come back. One woke up extremely angry at the doctor for being instrumental in re-establishing the life continuum.

The experiences were all connected with a very bright light, containing total awareness of the mind, but lacking a body. Each person was able to see their own body in the hospital bed and wandered off towards the bright light, quite aware of these occurrences, including watching the doctor at work. Then, removing themselves from the hospital and entering an area of bliss, happiness and great peace, some of them talked about beings they met. Most of them described one particular being which was "light." None of the descriptions had any religious symbolism in them but all of them were similar, some identical. With such books becoming more widely known the death moment has gained its rightful importance.

In the five daily recollections the Buddha asks us to remember that we are of the nature to die. At other times he talks about the fact that the last thought-moment is extremely important and consequently it is essential to get one's thoughts in order now. On one's deathbed it is too late. The wholesome aspects of our thoughts are always connected with loving-kindness, compassion, generosity and equanimity. If we arouse those in our minds now, as a habitual way of thinking, we can carry that with us to our deathbed. We are then assured not only of a favourable rebirth, at the very least, but also of harmony during our lifetime. This will make it possible for us to easily practise the Dhamma again. If we are born into a very poor family where nobody has enough to eat it will be very difficult to sit down to meditate because in a poor family everybody has to work to survive. If we are reborn in a society where meditation is unknown it will be very difficult to continue our practice. It is not wise, therefore, to wait till old age and death, but rather get our thinking process in order now. This entails knowing our thought-formation through mindfulness and attention.

Our appearance here is very short-lived—even seventy years is not very long. We can think of ourselves as a guest performer, always waiting for applause. Naturally that expectation makes life pretty difficult. First we have stage fright. Are we going to perform properly? Having given the performance, will applause be following? If we do not get it we feel devastated. Being a guest performer on this planet is a skilful way of thinking but waiting for the applause is the wrong view. If we know that we are doing the best we can with all our faculties, we do not have to wait for somebody else's approval. We can have right intention again and again. That is what matters most, because intention towards goodness concerns both oneself and others; less self-concern frees us to embrace others.

We must not fail in our Dhamma and meditation practice. Only if we have developed to some extent can we help others. Otherwise we act in ignorance (*avijjā*), which will not bring good results.

If we are concerned with our next rebirth we are really living in a dream. The person who is making the kamma now is not the one who is going to reap the results. The only connection will be the kammic residue, the result *(vipāka)*. Even this connection is very tenuous, because we can break the chain. If a person has made a lot of bad kamma and in the next rebirth makes much good kamma, the bad resultants may never fruit, and vice versa.

The case in point is Aṅgulimāla who killed 999 people and yet became an Arahant, because he became a monk under the Buddha and stayed in a monastery where his bad kamma didn't get a chance to fruit. However, Mahāmoggallāna, already an Arahant, was killed by robbers due to past kamma. We cannot establish a credit account of good kamma against all eventualities because we have no jurisdiction over the person who will inherit the kamma that we made in this life. But making good kamma now brings immediate results, joy and contentment for us and usually some happiness for others also. If one is able to give happiness to others we will also feel happy. It is useless to think about kamma made in a past life or to be made in a future life. None of us will know anything about the next life nor do we remember anything from our last life. Why worry about these then? Only this moment, right now, is important. The past is like a dream and the future is yet to come. When the future actually happens, it is always the present. Tomorrow never comes; when it does, it is called today. One cannot live in the future nor in the past. One can only live this single moment. If we really paid attention to every single moment, we would meditate well. We would also have no doubt about impermanence *(anicca)*. In fact we would see it so clearly that we could easily let go of our attachments, our clinging.

We could consider thus: "Have I used every moment to the best advantage?" If we have made some bad kamma in the past, we can quickly resolve to perform some good action. That is the only value the past can provide. Otherwise the most effective and compelling aspect of impermanence is that we are moving away from thought, speech and action so quickly, that we cannot even remember them, never mind hold on to them.

Yet we are trying to hold on to other people, to our ideas, views and opinions; we hang on to this body, to physical manifestations and mental aberrations and try to make them solid. It is impossible and cannot be done, there is only each moment. We can easily see in digital clocks how each moment comes and goes. Just watch a clock for five minutes, and realise five precious moments of your live are gone. The past is actually forgotten, except some highlights, but otherwise it has disappeared. That shows us with clarity that we are a flowing phenomenon without any substance. We are putting a substance into it, out of an ignorant appraisal of the totally untrue reality in which we are living. It is like a theatre, something we have made up ourselves, where people wear costumes and say their lines and believe this to be real life. We want to keep the theatre going but that is not possible and so everybody has dukkha, which cannot be eliminated through non-knowing or indifference, but only through a change of awareness and view.

Kamma-making is initially in the mind. Our mental formations make our kamma. Unless we become masters of our own minds we cannot escape from making bad kamma. The mind is constantly in danger of thinking something unwholesome. The negativities in the mind are innumerable: "I do not like it, cannot stand it; I'm afraid, it is boring…" All are negativities concerned with anger. "I want to get it, keep it, renew it," are also bad kamma, connected with greed. All arise in the mind.

Very few people watch their mind. They believe it to be difficult and tiring but it is much more tiring to make bad kamma because the results are heavy and unpleasant. Very few people have that inner buoyancy which denotes independent joy. Most people are bogged down by their mind's negativities, not by outer circumstances. Watching our own mind and making sure that we practise the four supreme efforts is the most beneficial thing we can do for ourselves and secures good kamma.

Out of our thoughts arise speech and action. We cannot talk without having thought it first and we cannot act without having made up our minds to do so. Although people speak and act so impulsively that they are not aware that a thought has gone ahead, that does not mean there was none. It just means that mindfulness and clear comprehension were lacking. The mind is the most precious asset we have. No jewel can compare with it, because the mind contains the seed of enlightenment. Unless we use the mind properly, we foolishly bury a jewel in the dirt. People often do so, primarily because they have had no training to do otherwise.

When we recognise that we have this most precious jewel of a mind, we will guard it from being scratched, bumped and dirtied, from losing its lustre and brilliance. Rather we make sure that the jewel of the mind remains pure and luminous and thereby make good kamma. The action itself, the Buddha said, is not of the foremost importance, it is the intention behind it. Even generosity can be extended from a wrong motivation. If the intention is to store up some merit for the future, that is rather selfish. If it is done out of compassion for those who have less, that is the ideal way. Yet, even with wrong motivation, it is still better to be generous than not. There is good kamma in it because one has let go of something that one owns.

The guard we keep on our mind will assure that whatever we do is done with right intention, the second step on the Noble Eightfold Path, which is our guideline. Kamma making depends on the mind, and the mind's purity depends on meditation. If we meditate diligently and regularly, eventually we will see with clarity what goes on in our mind. Some people are satisfied with gaining a little peace, but even that is already an advantage and growth aspect. If we watch the mind in meditation, we will learn to watch the mind also in daily living. Then we have a very good chance of making good kamma.

If we become tired of the ever-recurring cycle of loss and gain, praise and blame, fame and ill-fame, happiness and unhappiness—the eight worldly circumstances (*lokadhamma*)—we need to make a determined effort to shed clinging and craving. This effort has meditation as its base, but that is not all. Meditation is a means for gaining access to the ability to rid ourselves of the tendencies of greed and hate. The meditative process gives the mind the clarity to see these tenancies within ourselves, so that we can do something about them.

Our duty in this life as human beings with our senses and bodies intact, and being able to hear the true Dhamma, is to guard our mind and experience it in its natural state, which is pure, luminous, and pliable. Such a mind can reach the depth of the teaching where we find nobody that owns it.

VII. Spiritual Faculties

The Buddha spoke about five spiritual faculties which can turn into spiritual powers if we cultivate and develop them. We all have these faculties within us and developing them makes them powerful qualities which become factors of enlightenment. As long as they are only faculties, they are potentials for enlightenment.

The Buddha compared them to a team of horses with one lead horse and two pairs that are pulling a wagon. The lead horse can go as fast or as slow as it likes, the others have to fall into step with it. The pairs have to be in balance with each other, otherwise if one goes faster than the other the wagon will topple.

The leading spiritual faculty is mindfulness (*sati*). It is up to us how much of it we can find in any given moment. Mindfulness is a moment-to-moment mental factor which can be compared to an observer. If we have an observer with us all the time, it is more likely that we will stay on the path.

The first pair of spiritual faculties that has to be balanced is faith (*saddhā*) and wisdom (*paññā*). There is an analogy that the Buddha gave for these two qualities: He compared faith to a blind giant who meets up with a small, very sharp-eyed cripple, called Wisdom. The blind giant, named Faith, says to the small, sharp-eyed cripple named Wisdom: "I'm strong and can go very fast, but I cannot see where I'm going. You're small and weak, but have sharp eyes. If you will ride on my shoulders, together we could go very far."

This tells us that faith without wisdom, while being a strong faculty, is yet unable to find the right direction. We say "faith can move mountains," but being blind, faith does not know which mountain needs moving. However, when faith is coupled with wisdom there is enormous potential. The reason for such strength is that heart and mind are brought into harmony. The mind can have wisdom and the heart can have faith. When heart and mind are brought to a point of co-existence, of no separation, the power which develops is far greater than just $1 + 1 = 2$. It is more like 2 to the power of 2.

Faith as a quality in the heart has such great value because it is connected with love. We can only have faith in something or someone we love. Faith is also connected to devotion, which is a giving of oneself and a lessening of pride. These are valuable and necessary spiritual qualities. If we are devoted to a high ideal such as Buddha-Dhamma-Saṅgha, then we have the understanding that there is something greater than ourselves.

The devotion we can have for that ideal is manifested in giving our love and admiration, respect and gratitude, which are very important and helpful qualities to develop.

But the Buddha taught that blind faith is useless. Blind faith means that one believes what one is told without personal investigation, that one has faith in something that one's family adheres to, or because it has been written down in special books, because it has been transmitted from teacher to disciple, because it is something that one likes anyway, that promises some mystical revelation, or because the teacher is a respected person. All these are no reasons to follow a spiritual path. Do not believe because somebody told you so! But if there is some wisdom in the mind—and without wisdom life would be quite unbearable—we can quite easily investigate whether our faith and devotion are justified.

We can for instance, verify the first and second Noble Truths (*ariyasacca*) within ourselves many times in a day. If we do that, we know what these Truths mean; only believing them is not very helpful, because it will not make any difference in our hearts and minds. We can check out the impermanence and unsatisfactoriness of all worldly phenomena without much difficulty. Thereby we gradually gain more and more wisdom.

The unwavering faith in the Buddha-Dhamma-Saṅgha is one of the results that a stream-enterer *(sotāpanna)* gains when he or she has the first path moment, because until then the fetter of doubt still exists. If we have established unwavering faith within ourselves in the veracity and exactitude of the Buddha's teachings we have taken an important step. The heart quality within us will have opened up in a way which will be most helpful, but understanding has to go along. In Pali the one word *citta* denotes feeling and thinking, but in English we have to distinguish between heart and mind because we consider feeling a heart quality and thinking a mind quality, otherwise we cannot express what we really mean.

Our thinking capacity is rationality and logic, which is impaired by our emotionalism, by the reactions to our feelings. If our emotions are pure, as they are for example in devotion, gratitude, respect and faith, our thoughts have a much greater capacity for clarity. The impure emotions connected with passions of either wanting or not wanting are those which hinder our thinking capacity. We cannot think "straight" when we are under the sway of strong emotions. Our education system does not take any notice of that, nor do parents teach this to their children, yet the Buddha taught it quite clearly.

Each human being has a "male" and a "female" side. Just as the pairs of horses have to balance, both the male and female sides have to become a harmonious whole. The male side is usually connected to our rationality, logic, linear thinking, understanding. The female side is usually connected to feelings, nurturing, caring, compassion, love—all the emotional qualities. Each of us has both sides, the emotional and the mental capacity. Very few people develop both equally. Therefore their cart often topples. Emotionalism is just as much a danger as thinking without being in touch with one's feelings. Both can go very much astray.

In school we were taught to debate. We were given a subject to debate with another child. When we finished, we changed sides and were asked to hold the opposite view and debate, giving all factors of the other side. Any child can do it, any grown-up can do it. It is just straight-forward thinking. One can have the opposite opinion by the flip of a coin. There is no inherent truth in any opinion, because it is simply linear thinking. However, if these thoughts are connected to our feelings we can no longer debate the opposite side. This is the old story of having to bite into a mango to know its taste. We can be told many things about a mango. It is sweet, delicious, soft, but we cannot imagine its taste unless we get the feeling of the mango on our tongue and have the personal experience. Then we can no longer debate whether the mango is sweet or not, because we have experienced the truth. This is the difference between just thinking and thinking coupled with the experience of feeling.

A person who goes too far on the side of rational thinking has to learn to balance it with feelings, the female side. Anyone who thinks to the extent where the experience of feelings is hardly known has to practise much mindfulness of feelings. On the other hand, the female side is often emotionalism. This means we are carried away by our emotions and consequently our thinking is impaired. The quality of logical thinking, of delving into a thought process and being able to analyse, is not possible when the emotions are at the forefront. Of course in women this has a connection to the mores of the patriarchal society, but primarily it is due to the fact of not having developed one's potential for both sides, which is inherent in all of us.

The person who is primarily analytical is often under the impression that this will actually bring about all the desired results. Such a person, unless prodded and told often enough, will not try to get in touch with feelings. The one who is always relating and reacting to emotions is so habituated that he or she can no longer do anything else, until shown through the meditative process that there is an alternative.

If one lives only in relation and in reaction to one's emotions, life can become quite difficult. People who live like that often try to deaden their emotions as a way out of their dilemma. That is of course not the answer. The real answer is rather to purify the emotions. Naturally, the person who is a thinker also has to purify the emotions, but before such a person can do that, he or she first needs to get in touch with them. One who lives with emotions and reacts to them all the time also has to be in touch with them, but not to deaden them rather to encourage wholesome reactions. As the purification of the emotions takes place thinking will no longer be overshadowed by diffuse uncertainties. Unless we do that, we only use half of our potential. This is what faith and wisdom can mean to us, the emotions and the thinking. When we cultivate both, we develop our faculties into powers. Harmonising our emotional with our thinking capacities is the essence of harmonising faith with wisdom

A powerful mind is a great asset, but only in conjunction with purified emotions. Faith is one such purified emotion. Faith is much easier for people whose primary defilement is greed, rather than hate. Faith arouses pleasant feelings, which is greed's aim. In this case, greed is an asset, although basically it is, of course, a negative characteristic. But if we use it in a positive way we are engaged in a purification process, wanting that which is wholesome, which leads us to the supramundane.

First greed opens up into faith, resulting in pleasant feelings. Then we can use greed to want successful meditation, stream-entry *(sotāpatti)*, liberation. All are cravings, but they are going in the right direction, of using greed to get rid of greed. That is our best approach because greed is only truly eliminated by the non-returner (anāgāmi). If we use our craving in that manner, we are at least searching for that which will give us the greatest benefit, rather than searching for pleasure through the senses.

The Buddha's path is called "the middle path," which means a path of balance. We have to balance all extremes, so that they become a useful basis for a harmonious person, whose practice will flourish. This is one reason why the Buddha recommended the meditation on the loathsomeness of the body. People often say they do not want to think of their body as loathsome, it is a good working machine and very useful. But we are actually enamoured with our body; we are hanging on to it, loving it, trying to preserve it, keeping it young and beautifying it. We are attached to it and consider it "me." The loathsomeness of the body meditation is not designed to disgust us, but only to create a balance to our identification with our body. We can compare this with walking on a tight-rope; if we balance too far to the right, we fall down, too far on the left, we topple. Constant balancing is necessary, which has to be done by everyone for themselves.

If we know ourselves to be reacting to our emotions, we need to start analysing and inquiring into ourselves. It is difficult for someone who has always lived in reaction to their emotions to see beyond them. The meditation practice helps greatly, because the tranquillity that is bound to arise to some extent is conducive to penetration into reality. We need some self-knowledge, otherwise we cannot make any changes. Introspection and attention to our feelings and thoughts should provide enough insight into ourselves to lay the foundation for a meaningful change.

The other pair of spiritual faculties is energy (*viriya*) and concentration (*samādhi*). It is not physical energy that is needed, but rather mental energy, which has little to do with the capacities of the body. We need unwavering determination for this practice, which is transformed energy. The Buddha compared us with the man who is wearing a turban that is on fire. Obviously, if a man is wearing a turban that is on fire he is most anxious to get rid of it. That same kind of determination is needed to practise diligently. Energy is also dependent upon one-pointed direction. We realise what is most important and do not vacillate between social life, social action, practice, entertainment and the many other options open to us. Everybody has more energy for those things they like. We have to be very careful that we do not use up our energy searching for pleasant sense contacts because we like them. We have to be attentive to the fact that pleasant sense contacts are so short lived they will never give us complete satisfaction, and that we are using up our energy without getting any real fulfilment. So it turns into a waste of our energy.

If we see clearly through attention, mindfulness and introspection, that if we put our energy into meditation and practice of Dhamma, our dukkha is greatly reduced thereby and that we actually have a mode of living which includes everything else, then we will certainly turn in that direction. The rest of daily living happens anyway. Most people use up about 98% of their energy just to stay alive. Not that they have to work so hard to make a living, but just to attend to their daily duties and responsibilities, just to keep going. If our energy is used for meditation, mindfulness and bare attention, the mind faculties sharpen to the point where the minor things and duties necessary to stay alive are done in an easy and harmonious flow. We can start using our energy for that, which is most important.

If energy is not coupled with concentration it becomes restlessness. We can notice that in meditation; sometimes there is no concentration, yet there is a lot of energy. Then mind and body become restless; we would like to jump up and run away. If concentration is too strong and there is no energy, then the third hindrance (*nīvaraṇa*) arises, namely sloth and torpor. That is also easily noticeable in meditation. People who are used to concentrating and can do it well, may occasionally lack energy, and consequently concentration becomes conducive to sleepiness. When the mind is sleepy, the meditation should be directed towards insight, rather than calm.

Calm meditation which is purely concentration may result in sleepiness when there is not enough energy. But insight meditation, with attention on impermanence, the constant arising and ceasing of thoughts and feelings, may bring up the energy that is needed. As we only have a limited amount of vigour we have to use it in the best possible way. Most people do not realise that energy is a great asset and squander it on totally irrelevant activities. When we realise that it is essential for the spiritual path, then we may become more careful with it. As the body gets older, physical energy is reduced, but that does not have to include mind energy; on the contrary. When the body is young and full of vigour, a lot of physical activity may take place and the mind may be neglected. In a older person when body activity becomes less, the mind may receive most of the attention and mental energy could be increased.

Energy and concentration have to balance, primarily in meditation. When these faculties become powers, they result in the meditative absorptions. When wisdom becomes a power, it means insight into the three characteristics of impermanence (*anicca*), unsatisfactoriness (*dukkha*) and corelessness or non-self (*anatta*). When faith turns into a power, then it also manifests as the four immeasurable emotions (*brahmavihāra*): loving-kindness (*mettā*), compassion (*karuṇā*), sympathetic joy (*muditā*), equanimity (*upekkhā*). Mindfulness becomes a power when all four foundations of mindfulness (i.e., mindfulness of body, feeling, mind and thought-content) are habitually attended to. To become a master of all of these aspects is an ideal but to practise them is a necessity. Since all of us have these faculties within us there is every reason to cultivate them. When we have cultivated them we find ourselves more harmonious and balanced persons, with less difficulties, and capable of helping others. To develop these five faculties should be a primary object in our life. The balancing of them needs to be seen as connecting the heart with the mind.

VIII. Steps on the Way

There are three ways to approach the Dhamma.
One is by acquiring knowledge through study of the Buddha's discourses, trying to remember them as faithfully as possible. This knowledge is very useful for the propagation of the teaching through lectures and books.

The second way is through devotion, offering flowers and incense, reciting devotional verses, giving gifts and making merit. Generosity and meritorious action were highly recommended by the Buddha, but he didn't put any value on just being in the presence of monks and nuns. Once there was a monk who was so enraptured with the Buddha that he never wanted to be out of his sight. When this monk became sick one day and was unable to see the Buddha, he became despondent. The other monks asked him why he was so unhappy. He explained that he was depressed because he could not see the Buddha, who then came to visit the sick monk and said to him: "What do you see in this vile form? There is nothing to see in that. Whoever sees me, sees the Dhamma, whoever sees Dhamma, sees me."

The third approach to Dhamma, namely practice, has always been the one most highly recommended by the Buddha. He said a person with real reverence and devotion is one who lives according to the Dhamma. There are a number of steps to be taken when we approach the Dhamma through practice. The foundation would be moral conduct, meritorious actions, making good kamma. Without such a foundation, we do not have enough security within to be peaceful and at ease with ourselves, which are prerequisites for meditation.

This has sometimes been misinterpreted to mean that we should not meditate unless we have already complete purity of precepts and gained perfect mindfulness. But that does not follow, because it is meditation that helps us to gain mindfulness, and gives us insight into the efficacy of the precepts.

The next practice aspect is to guard our senses. This is frequently mentioned by the Buddha. It bears repeating and remembering. Without guarding our senses, we are always open to being tempted into wanting and craving, resulting in turmoil in the mind. Our sense contacts are triggers for lust and hate.

Our senses are so permanently engaged that we have lost sight of their impact, are taking all that for granted and think that is just the way it is. We also believe that what we see, hear, taste, touch, smell and think is really exactly as we are interpreting it. That is a fundamental error. Everyone experiences their sense contacts in an individual manner.

Here is an example: The food Westerners eat is considered baby food in Asia, while food spiced in the Asian way appears like hellfire to the Western palate. Even such a basic necessity as food shows up as a completely opposite experience. We can infer from that example that we all live in our own world. People argue vehemently because they believe their world must be the right one and even kill each other because of unresolved differences.

The Buddha was often asked such questions as: "Is the world finite or infinite, eternal or not?" His answer was: "What is the world? The world is our sense contacts." When asked questions such as these, the Buddha always brought the questioner back to practice. When we know that the world we live in consists of our sense contacts, we have something to practise with. When we know that the world is eternal or not, what is there to practise with?

Our senses include thinking, which is an almost constantly operating faculty. At this moment, we have touch, sound, sight and thought contact. Four of our six senses are engaged. Because our senses have been at work all our lives we believe that is the only way life can be experienced, which creates our deep craving to continue in this form. There is danger in this craving, something most people are not aware of consciously. Subconsciously we all know about it, because that is where our fears originate. If we examine ourselves for a moment we will realise that we harbour many fears, all carrying different names. Some people are afraid of spiders or snakes, some are afraid of the dark, some are afraid of airplanes, others that their loved ones may die, or that they might lose all their money. All sorts of different names for exactly the same fear; the fear of losing our identifications, the fear of unpleasant, painful sense contacts, ultimately the fear of annihilation. Yet losing this existence is a guaranteed outcome of being alive. It is just a matter of time.

These fears are caused by our attachment to our pleasant sense contacts, identifying with them and believing that apart from our senses there is no other reality. Naturally we want them to continue then. We take our unpleasant experiences in stride, expecting them to cease and the pleasant ones to arise again. If our unpleasant sense contacts are in the majority, then we say we are having a lot of dukkha. Or we might say: "I'm having a problem." As a matter of fact we are all having the same problem, namely that of not being enlightened. When we come to the realisation that our sense contacts are very momentary and their inherent satisfaction a matter of opinion, we will find it easier to let go of them during meditation.

Meditation will only happen when the sense contacts, particularly thinking, are suspended. If, for instance, the touch contact in the sitting position is recognised and attended to as unpleasant, the mind starts working on that. Remembering what someone said yesterday, last week or even ten years ago, can start the mind churning. This is all due to our attachment to our senses and our identification with them.

From all sense contacts feelings arise, there is no way that can be altered, but we can stop ourselves from reacting to such feelings, and believing that they belong to us. To get our meditation to a concentrated state, we must refuse to react to feelings arisen from sense contacts. The more we practise this in daily life, the easier it will be to become concentrated in meditation. We do not have to go along with this natural reaction of human beings. Meditative absorptions are supramundane and therefore require supramundane qualities in us. Whenever the Buddha described the way to Nibbāna he included the meditative absorptions as part of the practice, to lead us to the inner realisation of the Dhamma.

Guarding our senses is not only important in meditation, but equally valid in daily life. In a meditation course, where there is not as much input as in ordinary situation, it is a little easier to protect our minds from liking or disliking what we see, hear, taste, touch, smell and think. In order to facilitate this, we need to practise hearing only sounds, without explaining to ourselves what it is we heard. When the mind starts telling its story about the sound, at least we will know what we are doing, namely investing sound with a reality which gives it importance.

The same applies to eye contact. If, for instance, we are looking at a bush, our mind will say: "Oh, a cinnamon bush; who planted it? I wonder if we can use it?" Or any number of other ideas. Instead of all this, we can look at that which we call "bush" and be aware that our eyes are touching upon a form and thereby stopping the mind from making up stories. If we can manage to do this once or twice outside of meditation, we can use the same method of handling sense input in meditation. When we guard ourselves against the mind-made details of sense contacts, we are in less danger of falling into greed and hate. We will find this a great help in becoming concentrated in meditation.

Our lives are governed by our senses, but we do not have to continue with that. It is not compulsory. Within the operation of our six senses, it is not possible to find continued and unadulterated happiness. If it were possible, we would already be blissfully contented, since we have been having sense input day after day, life after life. The answer does not lie in improving our sense contacts, even though most people do try that, but rather in improving our reactions, so that eventually equanimity becomes our mode of living. This is the promise the Buddha made to us, namely, that we can get out of all dukkha, all problems. But we can not get out by having only wonderful sense contacts and not a single moment of unpleasantness. Such a thing has never been possible, not even when the Buddha himself was alive. But we can have moments when we are actually able to do just that. That one moment gives us the initial experience what it is like to be free, which is the only kind of freedom to be found in human life. There is no other. Anyone who understands the Buddha's explicit instructions, especially those who meditate, can practise in this manner.

The next step to be taken is mindfulness accompanied by clear comprehension (*sati-sampajañña*). Mindfulness is the mental factor of just knowing, clear comprehension the one of understanding. We need both. That too can and should be practised in daily life. Mindfulness of the body was praised by the Buddha as leading to the "deathless," a synonym for Nibbāna. When we watch our body's actions and realise that it can only follow the mind's instructions, this is our first step into insight.

Usually we take mind and body for granted. Most people are more interested in their body than in their mind and are looking after the body very well. Very few people are looking after their mind. Being aware of our body's movements gives us a chance to be alert without thinking, just knowing. Clear comprehension is our four-pronged mode of discrimination described previously.

We might think that such discrimination would slow us down unduly, that we won't be able to get our work done. Actually it has the opposite effect, because we will not do anything that is unnecessary. When we use mindfulness and clear comprehension again and again, they will become a habit, which will enhance our abilities to attain calm and insight. When we experience our mind ordering our body around, this is different from just knowing about it. We become intimately acquainted with our dual aspect of mind and body and can begin to investigate where is "me" in that. We may eventually find that "me" is our wish to be eternal, not to be annihilated.

Most people would like to experience calm, bliss and tranquillity in meditation. But those, whose minds are very active need to gain insight first in order to become calm. Those whose minds are more peaceful find it easier to become calm first and gain insight later. A little calm creates a little insight and vice versa. In practice we work on both these aspects to give ourselves the best chance to develop both simultaneously. When we watch the breath going in and out of the nostrils, we try to achieve a calm and peaceful mind. When the mind strays to thinking, we first realise "I'm thinking," and then see the impermanent nature of each thought, and how it so often rolls along without any purpose. This is a valuable insight, because we can infer that our thoughts are frequently not to be believed, are unimportant, have no solidity and do not provide a secure foothold for us.

Without such an experience, we might continue to believe all our thoughts and try using them as solid foundations for our life. When we see in meditation that we cannot remember what we were thinking from one second to the next that belief is shattered, never to arise again. When we start doubting our thoughts, this does not mean we start doubting ourselves. It refers to doubting our views and opinions, which is a most valuable practice.

In the Discourse on Loving-kindness (Karaṇīya-metta Sutta) an Arahat is described as being totally free from all wrong viewpoints (diṭṭhi). What the Buddha expounded to us were his own experiences. Viewpoints are always based on our wrong assumption that there is a "me" and are therefore discoloured by this underlying error. When we realise what our minds are up to, we will eventually stop having so many viewpoints and thereby let go of some of the mind's clutter. Most minds are full of ideas, hopes, plans, memories and opinions. Right and wrong are often based on culture or tradition and have no ultimate validity. They clutter up the mind and leave no space for a totally new outlook upon ourselves and the world.

An important step in this sequence is self-conquest, which the Buddha described as the way to Nibbāna. As long as we react to our feelings created through sense contacts, we must admit that we are "reactors" rather than "actors," victims rather than masters. We like to think of ourselves as more exalted than that, yet when we observe reality, that is all we can find. As soon as we have overcome this habitual reacting, we have taken a step towards conquering ourselves.

We do not force ourselves into unpleasant situations, which we haven't learned to cope with yet, because the mind will again react negatively, which does not help us on the path. We need not sit in excruciating pain in meditation, but we need to observe our mind and its activity. This will assist us also in daily living when unpleasant feelings and dislike arise because of words we hear or sights we see. When we learn to accept things the way they are, self-conquest has taken place which releases us from views and opinions.

Dukkha arises from the fact that we do not like the law of nature, to which we are subject. We do not like our loved ones dying, we do not like physical pain or lack of appreciation, we do not like losing what we prize. If we could just accept the way it is it would go a long way towards looking at the world more realistically, with less passion, which is the way to freedom. Our passionate desires keep us in bounds.

When we have the opportunity to sit quietly and watch ourselves, new insights about ourselves may arise. We are the prototype of impermanence but when our mind veers toward the past and starts rehashing old movies, it is time to turn it off. The past cannot be changed. The person who experienced the past, no longer exists, is only a fantasy now. When the mind strolls to the future, imagining how we would like it to be, we can let go by remembering the future has no reality either. When it happens, it can only be the present, and the person planning the future is not the same one, who will experience it. If we stay in this moment, here and now, during meditation, we can use that same skill in daily life.

When we handle each moment with mindfulness and clear comprehension, everything functions well, nothing goes amiss, our mind is content and inner peace can arise. Keeping our attention focused on each step on the way will eventually bring us to the summit.

IX. Pathways to Power

The four pathways to power are, according to the Buddha, essential aspects of realising liberation. He said: "If a monk or nun has missed the four pathways to power, they have missed the way to liberation. If they have practised the four pathways to power, they are practising the right way."

These four pathways are initially mundane, which means they are an endeavour which all of us are capable of pursuing. Only when they have become powers, are they supramundane and constitute four of the thirty-seven factors of enlightenment.

Because they are so essential to practice and cannot be disregarded, we need to know about them in detail. We have to understand them in an analytical way, so that we can check up on our own results. This is the criterion that eventually turns knowledge into wisdom. We can learn any of the Buddha's teachings by heart, that is not so difficult, but consequently we need to look at these teachings in the light of personal endeavour. We can check whether our practice has borne fruit or not. If so, we will continue in the same way as before; if not we need to alter our approach. By investigating within whether we are actually doing what the Buddha taught and whether it has become part of our own inner being, we gain insight into our mind's capacity. When we see that, through practice, we have been able to enlarge the abilities of our mind; we will not become complacent, but resolve to increase them further.

The four pathways to power start out with *chanda-samādhi*. *Chanda* means intention, and can be wholesome, unwholesome or neutral. It also means desire or direction. In order to make it a pathway to power we have to use it as the intention towards complete insight. *Samādhi*, as part of the term, means that the intention has to be fully concentrated and not dissipated. This would be the difference between living a worldly life or living a life wholly dedicated to spiritual endeavour.

In a worldly life we are forced to dissipate our intentions into different directions. It is the nature of life in the world. The necessity for obtaining and looking after many different objects, even though we can minimise that, will take up some time. There are always people and material aspects who have a claim on us. We have to honour those claims. Our own ambitions and desires are being fostered in the world as being useful and commendable. In order to cultivate "concentration of intention" leading to total liberation, we need to be in circumstances where no obstacles arise.

All four of the pathways have willpower as an adjunct. Concentration of intention also includes one-pointedness. It only becomes a true pathway when our intention is directed towards the greatest power of all, namely the power arising from letting go of all craving.

The second pathway is "concentration of energy," (*viriya-samādhi*). Everyone has a certain amount of physical energy which sometimes becomes detrimental to our mental endeavour when there is too much restlessness. If we have too little physical energy, that is also counterproductive. But mental energy can be increased, namely by being one-pointed, using our energy in one direction only, not having many irons in the fire. We need to be clear about what is of the utmost importance for us in this life. This needs checking up in the quiet introspection of our own contemplation. "What is it that I want most?" "Where do I want to expend my energy?" "What is my main intention?"

The answer may not be to come to the end of dukkha. That is all right too. But we can benefit by concentrating our energy and intention no matter where we are heading, as it will protect us from wasting our time with useless actions.

The willpower we can arouse depends very much on our insight. If we have seen the urgency of our own spiritual growth, we will find it easier to have the will for practice. All of us are subject to instinctual actions and reactions based on desire and craving. Willpower helps us to let go of these and direct our energy into different channels. Urgency (saṃvega) is an essential part of successful practice. When our insights give rise to seeing the whole world on fire from craving and ourselves burning with it, then urgency will become a natural part of our make-up and willpower a concomitant to it. Willpower arises in direct proportion to urgency, which is connected to our insight into the world around us; the world which does not stop at our front door, because it lives in our own heart and mind.

The next pathway to power is "concentration of consciousness," (citta-samādhi) or one-pointedness of concentration. When intention and energy come together in a powerful way coupled with willpower, meditative concentration can result. The first two pathways are causes for the third one to arise, leading to meditative absorptions. Deep tranquillity in one's meditation is the underlying factor needed for profound insights, which can change an ordinary worldling (*puthujjana*) to a noble one (*ariya*), which is the goal of our practice.

Most people today are not really aware of that goal, but are interested in meditation to gain release from stress. That too is all right. Why not? The Buddha's purpose and teaching were relief and release from dukkha once and for all, so that it can never arise again. If we translate dukkha as stress, which we can well do, then we might say, "Yes, it is relief from stress." But the kind of release the Buddha had in mind is based on the depth of insight, where we realise and experience that is not really dukkha that disappears, but the "me" who is experiencing it vanishes.

One-pointed intention and one-pointed effort lead to one-pointed consciousness. The mind finds itself in a state of awareness where there are no obstructions or obstacles resulting from thinking. Insight does not arise from thoughts, but is an inner, intuitive knowing quite different from discursive and logical thinking, rather an outcome of a clear and calm mind. This leads the awareness into the depths of truth, which has always been there, but which did not rise to the surface before, so that the mind could not grasp it previously.

What the Buddha experienced under the Bodhi Tree, when he was able to formulate the four Noble Truths and the Noble Eightfold Path, was not a result of discursive thinking nor of logical or learned understanding. It was a deep inner experience which arose from a totally calm mind without obstructions.

It is our saving grace that a mind can do only one thing at a time. When we are calm and concentrated all our hindrances (*nīvaraṇa*) are momentarily laid to rest. This is the boon of meditation. When there are no obstacles in the mind, it has the ability to recognise an entirely different depth than it does under ordinary circumstances, when we are always in danger of having greed, hate or deluded mind states arise. When we arouse the pathways to power we create a different dimension in the mind. This is essential, as otherwise we may believe in the Buddha and his teaching, but may not be able to prove it ourselves. It is up to all of us to live the Dhamma in heart and mind.

The fourth pathway is the "concentration of investigation." Subsequent to the experience of calm and tranquillity with their inherent expansion of consciousness, comes investigation for insight. The meditative calm becomes a condition for insight through concentrated investigation, when we realise the impermanence of even the best meditative states. None of the pathways, however, only apply to meditation. While they benefit us greatly in the context of meditation, they are useful and practicable in all other moments of our lives.

We certainly need concentrated intention in daily living. We cannot one day intend to be kind, the next day selfish, then kind again and expect to be peaceful and happy. We also need to know what we are aiming for in mundane living. If we want a university education, we have to concentrate on that intention. We cannot go to university one day, stay home the next day and expect to pass examinations.

Concentration of energy is also a basic requirement of daily living. If we conserve our energy to use it where it bears the best fruit, our mundane endeavours will flourish and be easily accomplished. If we develop and cultivate right intention, energy, willpower and concentration, we can increase our potential manifold.

Notwithstanding any results we may see in ourselves, we should never expect to be either totally perfect or totally imperfect. We need to look upon ourselves as practitioners, those who are learning. In the Buddha's time practitioners were called *sāvaka*, which means "hearer." If we consider ourselves in that way, we need not search for perfection or imperfection, but rather try to draw nearer to giving up all ideas of "me" and "mine."

Concentrated investigation of phenomena is an aspect of our moment to moment mindfulness, which enables us to see impermanence (*anicca*), unsatisfactoriness (*dukkha*) and corelessness or non-self (*anattā*) wherever we look. Everything that exits proclaims these three characteristics, so that we need never be without Dhamma consciousness. Usually one of the three aspects becomes more pregnant with meaning for us and our mind veers in that direction to investigate the underlying truth behind the reality in which we live.

We are never without an object for investigation. Our thoughts and feelings are full of these three characteristics. When there is a pleasant feeling, can we keep it? Do we feel unhappy when it is gone? Are we beginning to see this whole person we are so concerned with, as nothing but flux and flow, with no solid core to be found anywhere? When we look at ourselves again and again, we will eventually realise that we cannot find an unchanging substance within.

Depth of insight arises through the meditative process. However, we need to assist our practice by investigative thoughts and directions in daily living. If our mind is concerned with worldly affairs or sensual pleasures during the day, it is asking too much of it to become calm and insightful in the evening. It is an unrealistic expectation, which no mind can fulfil. We need to prepare our mind, so that it is used to thinking in terms of Dhamma consciousness, with mindfulness already established as a daily habit. Then we can proceed with meditation without first having to shed all mental burdens. We are already facing in the right direction and can easily achieve calm and peacefulness, which are our resource for mental energy.

When we are young, we may be inclined to think that our body is our source of energy. But the body can fall sick at any time, can be maimed or even die. Our real energy source lies in the fact that the mind can renew itself and become powerful through the arising of deep tranquillity. Then it does not matter whether the body is old and decrepit or young and healthy, because mind is the master and body the servant.

We need the meditative calm as our fuel supply. It is more important even than food. Although we eventually have to have food again, we can go without it for quite a long time, much longer than usually thought possible, and still have much energy to meditate. We have this natural resource within, yet very few people take advantage of it. In order to make use of it, the mind needs protection during daily living, so that it is already in the right frame of consciousness when meditation begins. Insight into the futility of ambitions and desires helps to lessen discursive and distracting thinking.

The four pathways to power are mundane when we are practising and become supramundane when we have perfected them. They bring total liberation from dukkha if the culmination of intention, energy, willpower, and calm and insight is achieved by us.

X. Making the Most of Each Day

Now the time has come to go home from this retreat. In order to take as much benefit as possible with us, we need to be aware how to organise our daily lives. If we go back and do exactly as we've always done, within a week everything will be forgotten. Coming to another meditation course in the future we would have to start all over again.

Who knows whether there is much time left in this life?. This is the only life for which we can take responsibility. Here we have some control over how we spend our day. The future is non-existent. "I'm going to meditate tomorrow" is foolish. There is no tomorrow, there is only now. When the next life comes, it is this life; actually this is our next life. Finding lots of reasons not to practise today is always possible: the children, the weather, the husband, the wife, the business, the economy, the food, anything will do. What kind of priorities we have is strictly of our own making.

If the future does not exist and the past is completely gone, what do we have left? A very fleeting moment indeed, namely this one. It passes quicker than we can say it. But by using each moment skilfully, we can eventually have moment-to-moment awareness, which results in deep insight.

When getting up in the morning the first thing would be a determination to be mindful. Becoming aware of opening our eyes is the beginning of the day and the beginning of mindfulness. If we have opened our eyes before becoming aware of that, we can close them and start all over again. From that small incident we will gain an understanding of mindfulness and what it means, then we can let the mind be flooded with gratitude that we have another whole day at our disposal, for one purpose only. Not to cook a better meal, not to buy new things but to draw nearer to Nibbāna. One needs enough wisdom to know how this can be accomplished. The Buddha told us again and again but we are hard of hearing and not totally open to all the instructions. So we need to hear it many times.

Being grateful brings the mind to a state of receptivity and joyful expectation of "what am I going to do with this day?" The first thing would be to sit down to meditate, maybe having to get up a little earlier. Most people die in bed. A bed is a perfect place for dying but not such a perfect place for spending an unnecessarily long time. If one has passed the first flush of youth one does not need so much sleep any more.

In most homes, starting at six o'clock, there is noise. If that is so we need to get up early enough to avoid that. That alone gives a feeling of satisfaction, of doing something special to get nearer to Nibbāna. If we have a whole hour available for meditation, that is fine; at least let us not practise under half an hour, because the mind needs time to become calm and collected. The morning hour is often the best for many people because during the night the mind is not bombarded with as many conscious impressions as it is during the day and is therefore comparatively calm. If we start meditating for half an hour and slowly increase it until we reach a whole hour that is a good programme. Each week we could add ten minutes to the daily practice.

After the meditation we can contemplate the five daily recollections as the mind now is calm and collected and therefore has more ability to reach an inner depth.

> I am of the nature to decay
> I have not gone beyond decay
>
> I am of the nature to be diseased
> I have not gone beyond disease
>
> I am of the nature to die
> I have not gone beyond death
> All that is mine, dear and delightful will change and vanish
>
> I am the owner of my kamma
> I am born of my kamma
> I am related to my kamma
> I live supported by my kamma
> Any kamma I will do, good or evil, that I will inherit.

The exact words do not matter that much. Words are concepts, only the meaning counts; the impermanence of our bodies, of what we think we own, such as people and belongings, and being responsible for our own kamma. Another recollection is about having a loving and kind attitude towards oneself and others and to protect one's own happiness and wishing to same for all beings:

> May I be free from enmity
> May I be free from harm

May I be free from troubles of mind and body
May I be able to protect my own happiness.

Whatever beings there are,
May they be free from enmity

Whatever beings there are,
May they be free from harm

Whatever beings there are,
May they be free from troubles of mind and body

Whatever beings there are,
May they be able to protect their own happiness.

Having reflected on these two aspects in a meaningful way, we can keep three things in mind. First comes mindfulness, bare attention to the prevailing mode of being. That can be a physical activity without the mind going astray or it may be a feeling or a thought which has arisen. Paying full attention, not trying to bury it under discursive debris, but knowing exactly what is happening in our lives.

When physical activity does not demand our attention, we can again direct thoughts to the fleeting aspects of our own lives and everyone else's, and reflect what to do in the short time available. When we consider this correctly, kindness, lovingness, and helpfulness arise as priorities. We need not help a lot of people all at once. Even helping one person is beneficial, maybe someone who lives in the same house It is the attitude and motivation that count, not the results.

Many people want to do some good but expect gratitude. That is spiritual materialism because they are aiming for a form of repayment for their goodness, at least a very nice future life. That too is equivalent to getting gain, not in the coin of the realm but through results. Both attitudes should be dropped and the realisation is to be established that "this is the only day I have, let me use it to best advantage." "What is most important, if I only have such a short time in this life?" Then we can act out of the understanding that in order to draw nearer to Nibbāna, we have to let go of self-concern, egocentricity, self-affirmation, personal likes and dislikes, because otherwise the ego will grow instead of diminish. As we affirm and confirm it more and more throughout this life, it gets bigger and fatter, instead of reducing itself. The more we think about our own importance, our own cares and concerns, the further away we get from Nibbāna, and the less chance for peace and happiness arises in our lives.

If someone has a very fat body and tries to go through a narrow gate, the body might knock against either side and get hurt. Likewise, if we have an extremely fat ego, then we might knock against other people constantly and feel hurt, the other people's egos being the gate posts against which we knock. If we have this kind of experience repeatedly, we get to realise that it has nothing to do with other people but only concerns ourselves.

If we start each day with these considerations and contemplations, we will tend towards not being overly concerned with ourselves but will try to think of others. Naturally, there is always the possibility of accidents.

Accidents of non-mindfulness, of not being attentive to what we are doing, accidents of impetuous, instinctive replies, or in feeling sorry for ourselves. These occasions have to be seen for what they are, namely accidents, a lack of awareness. There is no blame to be attached to other people or to ourselves. We can just see that at that particular moment we were not mindful and try to remedy it in the next moment. There is only the Arahant, who is fully enlightened, who does not have accidents of that sort.

The Buddha did not teach expression or suppression. But instead he taught that the only emotions which are worthwhile are the four supreme emotions *(brahmavihāra)* and that everything else needs to be noticed and allowed to subside again. If anger arises it does not help to suppress or to express it. We have to know that the anger has arisen, otherwise we will never be able to change our reactions. We can watch it arising and ceasing. However this is difficult for most people; anger does not subside fast enough. Instead we can immediately remember that to express anger means that particular day, which really constitutes our whole life, contains a very unfortunate occurrence and therefore we can try to substitute. It is much easier to substitute one emotion for another than to drop one altogether. Dropping means a deliberate action of letting go. As we have learned in meditation, we can substitute discursive thinking with attention on the breath; in daily living we substitute the unwholesome with the wholesome.

Usually our anger arises towards other people. It is not so important to us what animals do or what people whom we do not know do. Usually we are concerned with those whom we know and who are near to us. But since that is so we must also be familiar with some very good qualities of these people. Instead of dwelling upon any negative action of that person, we can put our attention on something pleasant about them. Even though they may have just used words which we didn't like, at other times they have said things which were fine. They have done good deeds and have shown love and compassion. It is a matter of changing our focus of attention, just as we learn to do in meditation. Until this becomes very habitual in meditation, it will be difficult in daily life, but diligent practice makes it happen. We practise in spite of any difficulty. If we remove our attention from one thing and put it somewhere else, that is all we need to work with. We will be protecting ourselves from making bad kamma and spoiling our whole day. We may not have another day.

The immediate resultants of all our thoughts, speech and action are quite apparent. If we keep our attention focused, we will know that wholesome emotions and thoughts bring peace and happiness, whereas unwholesome ones bring the opposite. Only fools make themselves deliberately unhappy, but since we are not fools we will try to eliminate all unwholesomeness in our thinking and emotions and try to substitute with the wholesome. All of us are looking for just one thing and that is happiness. Unhappiness can arise only through our own ideas and reactions.

We are the makers of our own happiness and unhappiness and we can learn to have control over that. The better the meditation becomes, the easier it will be, because the mind needs muscle power to do this. A distracted mind has no strength, no power. We cannot expect perfect results overnight, but we can keep practicing. If we look back after having practised for some time we will see a change. If we look back after only one or two days, we may not find anything new within. It is like growing vegetables. If we put seeds in the ground and dig them up the next day all we will find is a seed. But if we tend the seeds and wait some time we will find a sprout or a plant. It is no use checking from moment to moment but it is helpful to check the past and see the changes taking place.

At the end of each day it can be a good practice to make a balance sheet, possibly even in writing. Any good shop-keeper will check out his merchandise at the end of the day and see which one was well accepted by the customers and which stayed on the shelves. He will not re-order all the shelf items but only the merchandise that sold well. We can check our actions and reactions during the day and can see which were conductive to happiness for us and others and which were not. We do not re-order the latter for the next day but just let them perish on the shelf. If we do that night after night we will always find the same actions accepted or rejected. Kindness, warmth, interest in others, helpfulness, concern and care are always accepted. Self-interest, dislike, rejection, arguments, jealousy are always rejected. Just for one single day, we can write down all our actions on the credit or debit side, whether happiness-producing or not. As we do that, we will find the same reactions to the same stimuli over and over again. This balance sheet will give a strong impetus to stop the pre-programmed unwholesome reactions. We have used them for years and lifetimes on end and they have always produced unhappiness. If we can check them out in writing or see them clearly in our minds we will surely try to change.

Starting the day with the determination to be mindful, contemplating the daily recollections, realising that this is the only day we have and using it most skilfully and then checking it out in the evening on the balance sheet, will give us a whole lifetime in one day. If this is done carefully and habitually, the next day, which is our next life, has the advantageous results. If we've had a day of arguments, dislikes, worries, fears and anxiety, the next day will be similar. But if we have had a day of loving-kindness, helpfulness and concern for others we will wake up with those same modes of being. Our last thought at night will become the first one in the morning. The kamma we inherit shows up the next day, we do not need to wait for another lifetime. That is too nebulous. We do it now and see results the next day.

Before going to sleep it is useful to practise loving-kindness meditation. Having done that as the very last thing at night, it will be in our mind first thing in the morning. The Buddha's words about loving-kindness were: "One goes to sleep happily; one dreams no evil dreams; and one wakes happily." What more can one ask? Applying the same principles day after day, there is no reason why our lives should not be harmonious.

That way we are making the most of each day of our lives. If we do not do it ourselves nobody else will. No other person is interested in making the most of each day of our lives. Everyone is interested in making the most of their own lives. We cannot rely on anyone else for our own happiness.

As far as our meditation practice is concerned we must not allow it to slide. Whenever that happens we have to start all over again. If we keep doing it every day we can at least keep the standard attained in the retreat, possibly improve on it. Just like an athlete who stops training has to start all over again, in the same way the mind needs discipline and attention because it is the master of the inner household.

There is nothing that can give us any direction except our own mind. We need to give it the possibility to relax, to stop thinking for a little while and to have a moment of peace and quiet so that it can renew itself. Without that renewal of energy it decays just the same as everything else does. If we care for our mind, it will take care of us.

This is a sketch of how to use our day to day activity and practice. We must never think that Dhamma is for meditation courses or special days: it is rather a way of life, where we do not forget the impermanence and unsatisfactoriness of the world. We realise these truths within our own heart; just thinking about them is useless. If we practise every day in this way we will find relief and release from our cares and worries because these are always connected with the world. The Dhamma transcends the world.

Glossary

The following Pali words encompass concepts and levels of ideas for which there are no adequate synonyms in English. The explanations of these terms have been adapted from the *Buddhist Dictionary* by Nyanatiloka Mahāthera.

Anāgāmi—The "Non-Returner" is a noble disciple on the third stage of holiness, who has abandoned the five lower fetters.

Anattā—"No-self," or corelessness, non-ego, egolessness, impersonality, means that neither within the bodily and mental phenomena of existence, nor outside of them can be found anything that in the ultimate sense could be regarded as a self-existing real ego-identity, soul or any other abiding substance.

Anicca—"Impermanence," a basic feature of all conditioned phenomena, be they material or mental, coarse or subtle, one's own or external.

Anusaya—The seven "proclivities," inclinations or tendencies.

Arahat/Arahant—The Holy One. One who has liberated him- or herself from all mental fetters.

Ariya—Noble Ones. Noble Persons. One who has understood the Buddha's Teaching and is at least a stream-enterer (*sotāpanna*).

Ariyasacca—Noble Truth, i.e., the "Four Noble Truths," i.e., the Truths of Suffering (*dukkha*), the Origin of Suffering, the Cessation of Suffering and the Way Leading to the Cessation of Suffering.

Avijjā—Ignorance, nescience, unknowing, synonymous with delusion, is the primary root of all evil and suffering in the world, veiling man's mental eyes and preventing him from seeing the true nature of things.

Deva—heavenly being, deity, celestial. One of the divine beings who live in happy worlds, but are not freed from the cycle of existence.

Dhamma—The liberating law discovered and proclaimed by the Buddha, summed up in the Four Noble Truths (*ariyasacca*).

Diṭṭhi—View, belief, speculative opinion. If not qualified by "right," it mostly refers to wrong view (*micchādiṭṭhi*) and evil view or opinion such as that there is no harm in killing, stealing, etc.

Dukkha—(1) In common usage: "pain," painful feeling, which is bodily or mental. (2) In Buddhist usage as, e.g., in the Four Noble Truths (*ariyasacca*): suffering, ill, the unsatisfactory nature and general insecurity of all conditioned phenomena.

Jhāna—Meditative absorptions; tranquillity meditation. There are four jhānas, composed of different factors such as joy and equanimity.

Kamma—"action" denotes the wholesome and unwholesome volitions and their concomitant mental factors, causing rebirth and shaping the character of beings and thereby their destiny. In Buddhism the term *kamma* or *karma* does not signify the result of actions and most certainly not the deterministic fate of man.

Kammaṭṭhāna—"meditation subject," lit.: "working-ground" (i.e., for meditation) is the term for a subject of meditation, such as mindfulness of breathing, that is trained in.

Lokiya—"Mundane," are all those states of consciousness and mental factors arising in the worldling, as well as in the noble one, which are not associated with the supramundane.

Lokuttara—"Supramundane," is a term for the four paths and four fruitions.

Māra—The Buddhist "tempter" figure, the personification of evil and passions, of the totality of worldly existence and of death.

Mettā—Loving-kindness, one of the four sublime emotions *(brahma-vihāra)*

Nibbāna—lit. "Extinction," to cease blowing, to become extinguished. Nibbāna constitutes the highest and ultimate goal of all Buddhist aspirations, i.e., absolute extinction of that life-affirming will manifested as greed, hate and delusion and clinging to existence, thereby the absolute deliverance from all future rebirth.

Nīvaraṇa—"Hindrances," five qualities which are obstacles to the mind and blind our mental vision, and obstruct concentration, to wit: sensual desire, ill will, sloth and torpor, restlessness and worry, and sceptical doubt.

Papañca—"Proliferation," lit. "expansion, diffuseness," manifoldness, multiplicity, differentiation. This refers to the tendency of the mind to increase and proliferate on things observed through the senses.

Puthujjana—lit. "one of the many folk," worldling, ordinary man, anyone who is still not a Noble One, and possessed of all the ten fetters binding one to the round of rebirths, *saṃsāra*.

Sakkāyadiṭṭhi—Personality-belief, or the view of personal-identity, i.e., a permanent, self-same, truly existent being, is the first of the ten fetters and is abandoned at stream-entry.

Samatha—Tranquillity, serenity, is a synonym of *samādhi* (concentration). *Samādhi*, Concentration. A meditative state in which the mind is composed, unified and serene. See *samatha* and *jhāna*.

Saṃsāra—Round of rebirths, samsara. The cycle of rebirths by which beings, hindered by ignorance and fettered by craving, course on from one birth to the next, undergoing old age, sickness and death.

Saṅgha—lit. Congregation, is the name for the community of monks and nuns. As the third of the Three Gems and the Three Refuges, it applies to the community of the Noble Ones.

Saṃvega—a sense of urgency concerning the practice.

Saṅkhāra—formation. Mental formations and kamma formations. Sometimes: bodily functions or mental functions. Also: anything formed and created.

Sotāpatti—Stream-entry, the first attainment of becoming a Noble One, *ariya*.

Sotāpanna—Stream-enterer, one who has attained the first path and fruit and abandoned the fetters of personal-identity view (*sakkāyadiṭṭhi*), doubt (*vicikicchā*), and attachment to virtues and vows (*sīlabbata-parāmāsa*).

Vicikicchā—Sceptical doubt is one of the five mental hindrances and one of the three fetters, which disappears upon becoming a stream-enterer (*sotāpanna*).

Vipassanā—Insight into the truth of the impermanence, suffering and impersonality of all corporal
and mental phenomena of existence.

THE BUDDHIST PUBLICATION SOCIETY

The BPS is an approved charity dedicated to making known the Teaching of the Buddha, which has a vital message for all people.

Founded in 1958, the BPS has published a wide variety of books and booklets covering a great range of topics. Its publications include accurate annotated translations of the Buddha's discourses, standard reference works as well as original contemporary expositions of Buddhist thought and practice. These works present Buddhism as it truly is—a dynamic force which has influenced receptive minds for the past 2500 years and is still as relevant today as it was when it first arose.

You can support the BPS by becoming a member. All members receive the biannual membership book and are entitled to discounts on BPS books.

For more information about the BPS and our publications, please visit our website, or write an e-mail, or a letter to the:

Administrative Secretary
Buddhist Publication Society
P.O. Box 61
54 Sangharaja Mawatha
Kandy • Sri Lanka

E-mail: bps@bps.lk
web site: http://www.bps.lk
Tel: 0094 81 223 7283 • Fax: 0094 81 222 3679